Georgia Legal Research

Carolina Academic Press
Legal Research Series

Tenielle Fordyce-Ruff, Series Editor
Suzanne E. Rowe, Series Editor Emerita
❧

Arizona, Fourth Edition — Tamara S. Herrera

Arkansas, Second Edition — Coleen M. Barger, Cheryl L. Reinhart &
Cathy L. Underwood

California, Fourth Edition — Aimee Dudovitz, Sarah Laubach & Suzanne E. Rowe

Colorado, Second Edition — Robert Michael Linz

Connecticut, Second Edition — Anne Rajotte & Jessica Rubin

Federal, Second Edition — Mary Garvey Algero, Spencer L. Simons,
Suzanne E. Rowe, Scott Childs & Sarah E. Ricks

Florida, Fifth Edition — Barbara J. Busharis, Anne E. Mullins & Suzanne E. Rowe

Georgia, Second Edition — Margaret Butler & Thomas Striepe

Hawai'i — Victoria Szymczak, Cory Lenz & Roberta Woods

Idaho, Third Edition — Tenielle Fordyce-Ruff

Illinois, Second Edition — Mark E. Wojcik

Indiana — Ashley Ames Ahlbrand & Michelle Trumbo

Iowa, Third Edition — John D. Edwards, Karen L. Wallace & Melissa H. Weresh

Kansas — Joseph A. Custer & Christopher L. Steadham

Kentucky, Second Edition — William A. Hilyerd, Kurt X. Metzmeier & David J. Ensign

Louisiana, Fourth Edition — Mary Garvey Algero

Massachusetts, Second Edition — E. Joan Blum & Shaun B. Spencer

Michigan, Fourth Edition — Cristina D. Lockwood

Minnesota — Suzanne Thorpe

Mississippi — Kristy L. Gilliland

Missouri, Fourth Edition — Wanda M. Temm & Julie M. Cheslik

New York, Fourth Edition — Elizabeth G. Adelman, Courtney L. Selby,
Brian Detweiler & Kathleen Darvil

North Carolina, Third Edition — Brenda D. Gibson, Julie L. Kimbrough,
Laura P. Graham & Nichelle J. Perry

North Dakota — Anne E. Mullins & Tammy Pettinato Oltz

Ohio, Second Edition — Sara Sampson, Katherine L. Hall & Carolyn Broering-Jacobs

Oklahoma — Darin K. Fox, Darla W. Jackson & Courtney L. Selby

Oregon, Fifth Edition — Suzanne E. Rowe & Megan Austin

Pennsylvania, Second Edition — Barbara J. Busharis, Catherine M. Dunn,
Bonny L. Tavares & Carla P. Wale

Tennessee, Second Edition — Scott Childs, Sibyl Marshall & Carol McCrehan Parker

Texas, Second Edition — Spencer L. Simons

Washington, Second Edition — Julie A. Heintz-Cho, Tom Cobb & Mary A. Hotchkiss

West Virginia, Second Edition — Hollee Schwartz Temple

Wisconsin — Patricia Cervenka & Leslie Behroozi

Wyoming, Second Edition — Debora A. Person & Tawnya K. Plumb
❧

Georgia Legal Research

Second Edition

Margaret (Meg) Butler
Thomas (TJ) Striepe

Tenielle Fordyce-Ruff, Series Editor
Suzanne E. Rowe, Series Editor Emerita

CAROLINA ACADEMIC PRESS
Durham, North Carolina

Library of Congress Cataloging-in-Publication Data

Names: Butler, Margaret (Meg), 1973-author. | Striepe, Thomas, author.
Title: Georgia legal research / by Margaret Butler, Thomas Striepe.
Description: Second edition. | Durham, North Carolina : Carolina
   Academic Press, LLC, [2022] | Series: Legal research series | Includes
   bibliographical references and index.
Identifiers: LCCN 2022012045 (print) | LCCN 2022012046 (ebook) | ISBN
   9781531020026 (paperback) | ISBN 9781531020033 (ebook)
Subjects: LCSH: Legal research—Georgia.
Classification: LCC KFG75 .J64 2022 (print) | LCC KFG75 (ebook) | DDC
   340.072/0758—dc23/eng/20220525
LC record available at https://lccn.loc.gov/2022012045
LC ebook record available at https://lccn.loc.gov/2022012046

Carolina Academic Press
700 Kent Street
Durham, North Carolina 27701
(919) 489-7486
www.cap-press.com

Printed in the United States of America.

For my father,
a truly A-1 guy, and for my beloved and loving children.
My thanks for your encouragement and support.

To my wife, Jen,
who has been supportive throughout my career,
my children Jude and Arly,
who continually make me laugh,
and my parents, who have always been there.

Summary of Contents

Contents

List of Tables and Figures

Figures

Acknowledgments

Many thanks to Pamela C. Brannon, Faculty Services Coordinator at Georgia State University College of Law Library, for her enthusiasm for administrative law, accuracy, and her generous research assistance. Some day I, too, may have a favorite rule in *The Bluebook*. I appreciate the support of my colleagues who offered me encouragement and answered questions as I considered the topics of the manuscript. Thanks also to student assistant Hannah Kim and graduate research assistant Meri Elkin for their gracious assistance. Thanks to Annabel Wrightsman for her years of friendship and encouragement toward editorial excellence.

Thanks to all of my current and former colleagues at the University of Georgia Law Library for making me a better librarian and research instructor; and for their helpful advice in writing this book. A special thanks to Mikhael F. Thomson who assisted in researching various topics in this second edition.

Preface

We are very happy to share the second edition of *Georgia Legal Research* with you. The first edition authors, Nancy P. Johnson, Elizabeth G. Adelman, and Nancy J. Adams, set a high standard for process-oriented research training focused on Georgia law. We hope we have continued in their footsteps with this second edition.

This book may be used in a variety of ways. Because the book focuses on Georgia while also including federal context, it would be useful as a textbook in a general legal research course or even a Georgia-specific legal research course. A person engaging in independent, personal, or other academic legal research would find it helpful, as it contextualizes the Georgia and federal legal systems, the sources of law produced by those systems, and recommends processes for successful research.

In general, we believe that research is most successful under the following circumstances:

1) Research is undertaken with an understanding of the weight and authority of the sources of law;

2) Research is planned and organized; and

3) Research is validated and evaluated.

When researching in a new area, we recommend that researchers begin with secondary sources, as described in Chapter 4, then consider statutory law, if it exists, as described in Chapter 5. If the area of law is not governed by statute, we recommend turning from secondary sources to judicial opinions, as described in Chapters 6 & 7. Georgia and federal legal issues may require research in administrative law, such as when an agency has been charged with governing an area of law and has created regulations or enforces regulations. Such research, including the Georgia-specific complications and considerations, is described in Chapter 8. Researchers should remember to expand their research and validate their findings using citators, as described in Chapter 11, before calling a project complete.

We included chapters on additional topics including constitutions (Chapter 9), legislative history (Chapter 10), legal ethics (Chapter 12), and dockets and analytics (Chapter 13) because we thought they were important. These chapters may be included in a basic legal research course, or consulted as reference by someone who has a specific research question in mind and would benefit from any of those specific topics.

Constitutions are foundational, but research often does not begin with constitutions, as true constitutional issues are rare when compared with the frequency of legal issues arising from statutes, cases, and administrative law. Legislative history is important to research, but it is not necessary for every research project. Scholars may consult legislative history when making arguments about the interpretation of the law, and attorneys and judges may rely on legislative history when the language of a statute is not clear on its face. We included coverage of legal ethics due to their importance for attorneys and others, with descriptions of sources specific for both attorneys and judges in Georgia. In the practice of law, dockets are important, and legal analytics is increasingly important. Our final chapter provides context for students about the importance of dockets and how they are used, as well as a brief introduction to legal analytics.

We also included three appendices that we thought would be helpful. The first, Appendix A, describes in some detail legal citation as it typically appears in Georgia. Although the earlier chapters include descriptions of citation format, the Appendix gathers the information for a variety of sources in one location. Appendix B is a selected bibliography of resources that a person who wants to know more about the content of any of the chapters may wish to consult. Appendix C may be useful for those who just want to know quickly what Georgia-specific secondary sources may be useful in particular legal areas.

In this edition, we focused less on the use of the web and more tightly on the use of specific legal research tools available in print and online. At the time of publication, members of the Georgia Bar Association receive access to Fastcase as a benefit of membership. Georgia's Virtual Library, GALILEO, provides access to a variety of online resources, including Westlaw Campus Research, which may be helpful for legal researchers as well. It is worth contacting a local Georgia library to find out what resources may be available to you as you research. Additionally, many county courts in Georgia have law libraries researchers may visit. The metro Atlanta area counties offer online research tools for those who are able to come to the library in person.

We worked together to create this manuscript and consulted the first edition from time to time as we drafted this edition. Meg took the lead on Chapters 1, 3, 7, 8, 11, 12, and 13, while TJ took the lead on chapters 2, 4, 5, 6, 9, and 10. We drew heavily on the appendices of the first edition, particularly Appendix B. This shared endeavor has taken longer than we expected— thanks to an unexpected Spring 2020 semester—and we have supported each other well in this process.

Series Note

The Legal Research Series published by Carolina Academic Press includes an increasing number of titles from states around the country. The goal of each book is to provide law students, practitioners, paralegals, college students, and laypeople with the essential elements of legal research in each state. Unlike more bibliographic texts, the Legal Research Series books seek to explain concisely both the sources of state law research and the process for conducting legal research effectively.

Georgia Legal Research

Chapter 1

Research Process & Legal Analysis

After reading this chapter, you will be able to:

- Describe the process of legal research;
- Explain the role of legal analysis in the research process;
- Define types of legal authority; and
- Compare the organization of the Georgia and federal court systems.

I. Georgia Legal Research

Legal research in Georgia is similar to legal research in other jurisdictions, in large part because the process of legal research and analysis is similar across jurisdictions, even when the underlying resources consulted may vary by jurisdiction. Jurisdictions across the United States each have specialized resources or may require specialized knowledge about the legal landscape in order to efficiently and effectively research legal issues. This book will guide you through an overview of the legal research process and explain the role of legal analysis within that research process. The book also serves as a guide to the resources and strategies that you need to thoroughly and effectively research Georgia law. Federal research is also discussed throughout this book because researchers may need to find federal law that is also applicable in Georgia, to introduce additional resources, and to provide context.

Although this book includes information about individual resources, including books, databases, other resources, and their online iterations, the information provided is introductory rather than comprehensive. The resources and sources of law described in the book typically include information about "how to" use the resources or contain designated "help" or "FAQ" sections. Those tools are a researcher's best friend when it comes to ensuring efficient and effective use of the resources. This book, on the other hand, serves as a guide to finding Georgia resources that could be helpful or relevant and to understanding Georgia law.

II. Process of Legal Research: An Overview

Legal research is an iterative process because the steps of legal research are often repeated with a variety of sources. Typically, the process involves identifying the legal issue presented by the facts and the relevant jurisdiction(s). Then, planning the search; consulting sources, including secondary sources that explain the law, and primary sources that set forth the law in the controlling jurisdiction; and updating or validating the primary authorities to assure that they remain good law. When consulting sources in your research, researchers may choose to browse, search, or do a combination of both. Researchers often follow the process described in Table 1-1 when faced with a question in an area of law that is unfamiliar. These steps are described more fully in Chapter 2 about research planning, documenting, and organizing.

Table 1-1. Legal Research Process

Legal Research Process: Efficiency Considerations
Think in advance of searching
Identify the goal of your search—is it an explanation of an area of law? An explanation of a narrow legal issue? A specific statute or case?
Plan your search—identify concepts, synonyms, antonyms, terms of art, group terms, etc.
Plan the type of search—is it simple or advanced? Do you need specific connectors for concepts?
Search in a database that contains the type of material that matches your search goal
Evaluate whether your search results are on point with the goal of your search; if necessary, revise your search to reflect needed changes

To be effective, researchers often identify their research goal at the beginning of the research in the planning stage. Articulating the desired goal makes researching easier for two reasons. First, it is easier to know where to look for information when you know the type of information you seek. Second, it is easier to recognize that you have found relevant law when you have a clear understanding of what you need to accomplish.

III. Legal Analysis in the Research Process

The basic process of legal research seems straightforward in the abstract. However, legal research becomes more complex in practice because legal analysis is required throughout the process. Without legal analysis, the researcher is at a loss, with no legal issue to explore, no legal concepts or terms of art to guide the search.

Researchers engage in legal analysis when implementing their research plans. Researchers will define their legal issues, search secondary and primary sources to identify relevant law from controlling jurisdictions, and validate the law identified. At all stages, researchers engage their analytic skills. Table 1-2 lists the recommended steps of the research process. These steps for effective research complement the steps of legal research process that are listed in Table 1-1. Researchers find it helpful to apply the steps for effective research at each stage of the legal research process.

Table 1-2. Steps for Effective Research

Legal Research Process: Basic Workflow
Familiarize self with facts; identify jurisdiction
Consult secondary sources to get background in area of law
Identify controlling primary sources, starting with constitutions, statutes, and regulations (if any), turning at end to case law
Update primary authorities
Answer any additional or related question(s) that may have arisen during the search
Stop when analysis is fully supported, all authorities are valid, and searching turns up the same (already discovered or known) resources

Researchers also rely on their analytical skills when searching (by index in print or text searching online) or browsing. When reviewing the sources found by consulting an index or the results of a text search from a database, the researcher must evaluate the sources or results for relevance to the legal issue. Similarly, when browsing, the researcher must be thinking critically about the information as well as the structure and organization of the resource being consulted to evaluate the best browsing path to identify relevant information.

IV. Types of Legal Authority

Legal authority is typically divided into two large categories: secondary and primary authority. *Secondary authority* refers to other legal sources that explain the law or help to locate or find the law. Included among secondary authorities, also called secondary sources, are treatises, law review articles, legal encyclopedias, and digests. Secondary sources are described in Chapter 4.

Primary authority refers to the sources of law produced by government bodies with law-making power. Each branch of government produces law, with the legislative branch producing statutes, the judicial branch producing judicial opinions, and the agencies of the executive branch producing rules or regulations, and administrative decisions.

Within the category of primary authority, the distinction between mandatory and persuasive authority is critical to researchers. *Mandatory authority* refers to the laws that are binding or controlling in a conflict. This may be described as the law of the controlling jurisdiction. For example, in a conflict arising under the law of Georgia, mandatory authorities would include Georgia's Constitution, the statutes enacted by the Georgia legislature, opinions of the Supreme Court of Georgia, and Georgia administrative rules. Opinions by the Georgia Court of Appeals would bind the trial courts within the appellate court's jurisdiction. *Persuasive authority* is usually thought of as the law of another jurisdiction. In a conflict arising under the law of Georgia, the law of Florida or another state—whether statutory or common law—would be considered persuasive. These persuasive authorities, whether the law of another jurisdiction or secondary authorities (not the law) are most often cited based on the quality of their reasoning, analysis, and relevance.

In addition to analyzing whether authority is mandatory or persuasive, a researcher also must consider the weight of authority. The law of Georgia derives its authority of the Georgia Constitution, just as federal law derives its authority from the United States Constitution. The weight of authority may be seen as a hierarchy, with the jurisdiction's constitution at the apex, followed by relevant statutory authority and then by relevant administrative rules, if any. Determining the authority of cases is more complex.

The courts, through judicial opinions, interpret statutes and regulations, following the laws unless they conflict with the jurisdiction's constitution. Judicial opinions must follow regulatory authority unless the agency, in the rule-making process, exceeded the scope of authority delegated to it by the legislature or failed to follow the steps required for rule-making. Once opinions, issued by judges, have interpreted statutes or regulations, those opinions elaborate further on the way in which the statutes and regulations are to be applied. Assuming the opinions are from your jurisdiction, the opinions would also be controlling in the area of law. *Common law*, or law made by judges, only rises in its weight, however, in areas in which there are no controlling statutes or regulations.

For a variety of reasons, researchers should begin their research by consulting secondary sources, then turning to primary sources. When consulting primary sources, researchers should consider first constitutional issues, and then consult statutes and regulations (if any), before turning to case law.

V. Court Systems

Although judicial opinions are often not at the apex of the hierarchy of primary sources, researchers must often read judicial opinions to make sense of the law. To fully understand these opinions, let's review the basic court system. In both the federal and Georgia contexts, the highest court—the court of last resort—is called the Supreme Court. A matter is typically heard by the Supreme Court only after it has first been heard at the trial court level and then been the subject of an appeal to an intermediate court of appeals.

A. Georgia Courts

Georgia has three types of trial courts. There are *courts of limited jurisdiction*, which means the courts are only able to hear particular types of matters. Some courts are limited by subject matter, such as the probate and juvenile courts, which handle administration of decedents' estates and juvenile delinquency or abuse-related matters respectively. Georgia voters amended the Constitution in 2018 to establish a new type of court. The State-wide Business Court has jurisdiction over particular types of claims, such as those arising under specific business laws and involving more than $500,000 or $1 million in damages, depending on the type of claim asserted. Other Georgia courts are limited by the scope of their coverage, such as state courts which are limited to the jurisdiction of their county, magistrate courts, which are limited to civil claims under $15,001, or minor criminal offenses, and municipal courts, which handle traffic offenses and other issues arising under local ordinances.

The third type of court are courts of general jurisdiction. Superior Courts of Georgia have broad civil and criminal jurisdiction, including divorce and felony trials and also may, in the event of error, correct limited jurisdiction courts. These courts are organized into circuits, and each court represents one or more counties. Superior Courts in the metro Atlanta area may join the Metro Atlanta Business Case Division, which considers complex commercial and business cases. The Metro Atlanta Business Case Division was formerly known as the Fulton County Superior Court Business Court Division, but rules have expanded its scope and changed its name.

The Court of Appeals of Georgia and the Supreme Court of Georgia are the courts of review. The Court of Appeals provides first review for some trial court decisions, with the goal of correcting legal errors made at the trial level. The court has 15 judges who serve on three-judge panels. A decision by a three-judge panel may be reviewed by the full court. Similarly, the Supreme Court of Georgia reviews decisions made by lower courts. It is able to pass judgment on the constitutionality of state statutes, death penalty criminal sentences, and it selectively reviews opinions by the Court of Appeals.

Not every trial court judgment in Georgia is eligible for appeal to the Court of Appeals. The scope of the right of appeal is addressed by the Official Code of Georgia, which lists fourteen types of matters in which a party seeking appeal must generally seek permission to appeal, or *certiorari*, which is selectively granted.[1] However, some matters do have an automatic right of appeal.[2]

Further, Georgia trial court opinions are not generally published in print. They may be available directly from courts or through premium legal research databases. Georgia trial court opinions are not designated as published and are not mandatory law. However, opinions issued by the Metro Atlanta Business Case Division may be found archived at the Georgia State University

---

1. O.C.G.A. § 5-6-35 (2021).

2. The rules governing direct appeal in Georgia are complicated. O.C.G.A. §§ 5-6-34 and 5-6-35 set forth the basic rules. However, to fully understand the rules, researchers would benefit from consulting a secondary source such as Christopher J. McFadden et al., *Georgia Appellate Practice* (2021–2022 ed.).

College of Law Library website.[3] Appellate court opinions, on the other hand, may be designated for publication by the Court of Appeals and those opinions have precedential value. Georgia trial courts are required to follow Georgia appellate court opinions that have precedential value, which means that other courts are not required to follow them. Chapter 6 further discusses the differences between opinions that are designated for publication and opinions that do not receive this designation.

B. Federal Courts

In the federal context, the United States District Courts conduct trials, make findings of fact, and issue conclusions of law. The findings of fact and conclusions of law are described as the opinion of the court, or the judgment. At the trial court level, these opinions are often available through the clerk's office. However, some of these decisions are available in Lexis, Westlaw, or in a print publication published by West entitled *Federal Supplement.*

The system includes 94 district courts, and the district courts generally reflect state boundaries. Some states, such as Georgia, have several district courts. Georgia has the southern, middle, and northern districts. You will find Savannah in the southern district; Macon and Athens in the middle district; and Atlanta in the northern district. Other states, such as South Carolina, form a single district with no further subdivision.

Additional federal trial courts include the bankruptcy courts, the Court of International Trade, and the U.S. Court of Federal Claims. All bankruptcy cases must be filed in federal courts, and each federal district has a U.S. bankruptcy court. Bankruptcy court opinions are published in the *Bankruptcy Reporter.* The Court of International Claims considers only cases related to international trade and customs law, and the opinions are currently published in a variety of reporters including the *Court of International Trade Reports* and the *Federal Supplement.* The U.S. Court of Federal Claims considers claims seeking money damages from the U.S. government, and its opinions are currently published in the *Federal Claims Reporter.* The U.S.

---

3. Georgia State University College of Law Library, *Georgia Business Court Opinions,* https://readingroom.law.gsu.edu/businesscourt/ [https://perma.cc/9CE6-FFCL].

Courts of International Trade[4] and of Federal Claims[5] are special because appeals from those trial courts are heard only by the Court of Appeals for the Federal Circuit.

An appeal from a federal district court is generally heard by a United States Court of Appeals. There are twelve regional circuits, and each circuit has one appeals court that hears appeals from any lower courts within the circuit. Lower courts include bankruptcy and district courts. The thirteenth federal appellate court is the Court of Appeals for the Federal Circuit, and it has nationwide jurisdiction over particular types of matters including appeal of intellectual property decisions of lower courts or administrative agencies.[6]

Unlike the trial court opinions issued by Georgia Superior Courts, many trial court opinions from federal district courts are published, both in print and on the free web. Those opinions are not precedential, because no court is required to follow them. Similarly, opinions issued by the federal courts of appeal are only precedential when they are designated as such by the court, even if the opinions are available in print or on the free web.

C. Courts of Other Jurisdictions

Courts in other jurisdictions, or states, do not all have the same name and organizing structure for their courts. For example, in New York, the Supreme Courts are the trial courts. In Texas, there are two different courts that are the highest for their respective subject matter: The Court of Criminal Appeals and the Supreme Court.[7]

---

4. *About the Court*, United States Court of International Trade, https://www.cit.uscourts.gov/about-court [https://perma.cc/9DFZ-R8VD].

5. *The People's Court*, United States Court of Federal Claims, http://www.uscfc.uscourts.gov/sites/default/files/USCFC%20Court%20History%20Brochure_1_0.pdf [https://perma.cc/42M5-EUMA]

6. *Court Jurisdiction*, United States Court of Appeals for the Federal Circuit, http://www.cafc.uscourts.gov/the-court/court-jurisdiction [https://perma.cc/JLY5-XAX].

7. *About the Texas Courts*, Texas State Law Library, https://www.sll.texas.gov/the-courts/about-the-texas-courts/ [https://perma.cc/F7JQ-SNMP]. For helpful information about state court structure in general, consider consulting the Court Statistics Project, a joint project of the Conference of State Court Administrators and the National Center for State Courts. Their site is http://www.courtstatistics.org/ [https://perma.cc/F8E6-CTGW].

VI. Conclusion

The research process includes common steps across jurisdictions, beginning with understanding the facts and identifying the law that applies. Generally, researchers begin with secondary sources, consult primary sources starting with constitutions, statutes, and regulations before turning to case law, and update the primary sources. Researchers benefit from following recommended steps for effective research including pausing to think about legal issue before searching and taking notes regarding search results.

Researchers analyze primary and secondary source materials and their relevance to legal issues throughout the research process. Understanding the levels of courts and the weight of cases in the Georgia and federal court systems facilitates research.

Chapter 2

Planning, Documenting, and Organizing Research

After reading this chapter you should be able to:

- Identify the elements of a research plan;
- Draft a research plan;
- Recognize the value of using a research log; and
- Explain how to organize your analysis.

I. Preparing to Research and Organize Results

This chapter focuses on the steps researchers need to take prior to beginning their research in order to be efficient. The chapter also discusses the importance of documenting and organizing your research. Chapter 1 provided an overview of the entire research process. This chapter will focus on the preliminary planning.

Before beginning research, whether it is for a client, an institution, or otherwise, the researcher needs to understand the research assignment. The time it takes to do this preliminary analysis will depend on the researcher's familiarity with the legal issue. If the legal issue is centered on a legal topic that the researcher encounters frequently, then this preliminary analysis will be limited. However, if it is a new legal topic for the researcher, the researcher may need to dedicate a substantial amount of time to gain a basic understanding of the legal topic before commencing the research on the specific legal issue or issues. There are three parts to this preliminary analysis:

A. Questions

When first getting a research assignment, it is important to ask questions to fully understand the assignment. The questions asked may vary depending, for example, on whether a client or a supervisor requested the research. These questions can solicit information about:

- Jurisdiction;

- Legal topic or issue;

- Terms of art to be used in searching;

- Any important secondary sources, statutes, cases, or administrative materials to consult;

- Fundamental characteristics of the client (i.e. marital status, age, type of entity, etc.);

- Significant facts of the legal issue;

- Any constraints on time, money or individuals to consult;

- Type of work product that is to be produced; and

- Due date.

B. Formulating the Preliminary Legal Issues

The next step in the preliminary analysis is to formulate the legal issues that will be researched. As discussed in Chapter 1, legal research is not a linear process. As a researcher moves through the legal research process, she may discover previously unknown legal issues that apply to the factual situation. However, prior to commencing research, the researcher needs to clearly define the (initial) legal issues. This will ensure that the researcher is concentrating on resolving the specific legal issues that apply, and the researcher will not waste time branching out into inapplicable issues.

C. Preliminary Research

Before formulating the legal issue and preparing the research plan, a researcher may need to perform some preliminary research to gain background on the legal topic. This preliminary research informs the researcher about potential claims, defenses, legal issues, significant facts to consider, and terms of art.

This preliminary research can be done in a variety of ways: through discussion with other legal professionals, reviewing similar files, by consulting secondary sources such as legal encyclopedias or continuing legal education materials, or general internet searching. The researcher is not trying to find an answer to the legal issue at this point. The researcher is trying to obtain sufficient knowledge about the legal topic to recognize potential issues, understand the key areas and types of law that apply, and to assist in generating search terms.

II. Research Plan

A *research plan* is defined as "a strategy for finding information on an identified [legal issue]."[1] Although some researchers prefer to have a written plan indicating the steps of their intended research paths, there is no requirement that a research plan be written. Most important is the thinking and analysis of the planning process. Many legal researchers find it beneficial to use a written plan to focus their thinking about the research project before reviewing relevant primary and secondary sources. These written plans can be as formal or informal as the researcher requires. The main goal of the research plan is to ensure researchers are conducting their research in an efficient and thorough manner, but there are many other benefits to preparing a research plan.

A. Benefits of a Research Plan

1. Pausing to Think

One of the biggest benefits of a research plan is the opportunity for the researcher to think about the legal research process before logging into a legal database or searching for relevant materials in print. By pausing and considering the significant facts, legal issues, jurisdiction, search terms, and potential sources, the researcher may efficiently locate the answers to the legal issue. The research plan allows the researcher to search intentionally, rather than randomly following rabbit trails. The time spent clarifying the legal issue and determining what is sought makes it easier for the researcher to evaluate search results as to whether they are helpful or not, further focusing the research process.

---

1. Caroline L. Osborne, *The Legal Research Plan and the Research Log: An Examination of the Role of the Research Plan and Research Log in the Research Process*, 35 L. Ref. Serv. Qtly 179, 179 (2016).

2. Saving Money

The research plan saves money for the researcher's institution and/or client. Conducting research in commercial databases is expensive, and at least a portion of the time spent on conducting research for a client will be billed to them. Due to planning, the researcher is more efficient during the research process. The research is more focused on the legal issues to be resolved. The sources consulted are the most appropriate legal resources to consult, rather than too broad or too narrow. Researchers will not be wasting their time on irrelevant issues or conducting searches that bring about unrelated results. This ultimately saves money in terms of researcher time and may further produce lower charges for use of premium databases.

3. Completeness

Researchers avoid the risk of overlooking or missing sources by planning their research process. Researchers may need to consider state, federal or local (or all three) jurisdictions. Researchers may need to consider only cases, or researchers may need to consult statutes and regulations as well. By thinking through the legal issues and the needed end product, the researcher gains confidence that all necessary research steps have been taken.

4. Record

The research plan provides a record of the research strategy. This is different than the research log, discussed below, which tracks the actual research. This research plan provides a memo that other legal professionals can review to see the researcher's strategy. This permits other legal professionals to make suggestions about different terms to use or other secondary sources to consult, ensure that the proper jurisdiction was selected, and confirm that the proper legal issue was researched. This record is also important as a document in a legal file. When other legal professionals are reviewing a file, they can see the path the researcher used and will be able to easily determine if anything was overlooked in the research process.

B. Essential Elements

There is no "one" form for a legal research plan. There are a variety of examples[2] that researchers can use to create their own template, and there is

---

2. Robert M. Linz, *Research Analysis and Planning: The Undervalued Skill in Legal Research Instruction*, 34 L. Ref. Serv. Qtly 60 (2015), scholar.law.colorado.edu

a template attached as Appendix 2-1 at the end of this chapter. Researchers can formulate their research plan template as best suits their needs and can modify the template as needed for each research project. Following are elements to consider in developing a legal research plan.

1. Facts

The research plan should contain the significant facts relevant to the legal issue. Significant facts include the facts that will ultimately determine the outcome of the legal issue and the facts necessary to give a third-party some context about the matter.

There is no magic method for determining which facts need to be included or excluded as part of a research plan. The main goal of this planning stage is identifying facts necessary to locate the relevant and controlling law, to facilitate later analysis. Note that as research progresses, it is possible that legal information identified provides new perspectives about facts, shifting some information from legally insignificant to legally significant.

In this section, researchers should focus on what information or facts are necessary to understand the legal problem they are trying to resolve. One of the best techniques to do this is to consider the five Ws & H: Who, What, When, Where, Why, and How. Table 2-1 provides examples of the different facts researchers should consider when drafting the fact section.

Table 2-1. Generating Research Terms

Question	Examples
Who is involved?	individual, trust, government entity, child, property, invitee
What happened?	injury, crash, contract dispute, seeking injunction, theft
When did it occur?	date, time of day, age of parties, during a storm
Where did it occur?	public area, commercial establishment, residence, outside, government building
Why did it occur?	negligence, intentional act, contract was silent, goods were not delivered
How did it occur?	breach by a party, machine defect, individual was not paying attention

---

/cgi/viewcontent.cgi?article=1153&context=articles [https://perma.cc/3AWP-FX2C]; Osborne, *supra* note 1.

2. Legal Issue(s)

The legal issue section of the research plan is probably the most important section. If a researcher is not researching the correct issue, or has not clearly defined it, then it will be impossible to be efficient in the research.

Researchers may certainly find additional issues as they move through the research process, but it is essential to be researching the correct issues prior to commencing the research. It is helpful to discuss the issues with your supervisor or other legal professionals if you are dealing with a new legal topic.

There could be multiple legal issues to research for one project, and do not forget about threshold issues as well. These could include standing, statute of limitations, jurisdictional, choice of law, and other legal questions that need to be resolved before getting to the substantive legal issues at hand. Also, researchers may find that answering one legal issue or question raises a follow-up question.

3. Jurisdiction

The research plan should state the jurisdiction's primary law which will apply. This could certainly devolve into a legal issue if there are choice of law questions. This section should clearly provide what law applies: state, federal, or both, and the applicable state. In some instances, consideration of local law may also be necessary.

4. Potential Search Terms

Identification of search terms is helpful whether the researcher is browsing a table of contents, consulting an index, or creating a keyword search to use online in a free or premium legal database.

One approach to the development of terms is to identify the relevant concepts by considering the relevant facts and listing the concepts. Then the researcher considers each concept in turn, exploding the concept by adding synonyms or related terms. For example, when researching the law related to goat bite injuries, one concept is the goat (a Who/What). Possible search terms for that concept include kid and animal.

Concepts may be broadened or narrowed by category, like goat and animal. Another way to broaden or narrow a concept is by considering synonyms and antonyms. When searching for car, possible synonyms include automobile, vehicle, and truck. Consider abstractions of a word as well, for example Facebook is a concrete term while social media, internet, and web are abstract terms that may include Facebook.

Listing the potential search terms provides the researcher with a collection of legal words, phrases, and terms of art that can be used when conducting her searches. These terms should be comprised of words relating to the legal issues as well as the legally significant facts. At this point the researcher is only brainstorming and does not need to be concerned whether a word is ultimately used as part of a search.

5. Potential Sources

This section is helpful for novice researchers. It acts as a checklist to remind a researcher to review relevant secondary and primary materials before finalizing the research. If the researcher knows of specific secondary sources, statutes, cases, or administrative materials that need to be reviewed prior to completion, they should be listed in this section.

However, if it is a topic that is new to a researcher, she can just provide a list of general resources to consult. For example, if the research involves whether an employer must pay workers compensation to a Georgia resident who was injured when not wearing a safety harness, then some potential general resources would be: (i) a Georgia legal treatise on employment law or a Georgia legal treatise on workers compensation; (ii) Georgia statutes on workers compensation; (iii) Georgia/Federal regulations on safety harness requirements; and (iv) the Occupational Safety and Health Administration's website.

6. Miscellaneous

This section captures the fundamentals of the research project. This includes when it is due, what format the final product should be in (memo, list of cases, e-mail, copy of relevant statutes, etc.). It can also include items such as time limitations, the overall goal of the client, cost constraints on research, other relevant files, etc.

III. Tracking Your Research

When the research planning has been completed and you start to research in earnest, it is important to track your research. Even with electronic research tracking available through Fastcase, Lexis, and Westlaw, researchers benefit from tracking their research in one log that comprehensively tracks all the research performed, whether it was done in different legal databases, print, internet searching, or otherwise. Researchers can track their research using paper and pen, word processing documents, spreadsheet files, and client management systems. Tracking research becomes even more important when managing several research projects at the same time. Researchers may find it helpful to take advantage of tools to track and sort research by client matter.

Just like a research plan, a research log can take whatever form is most useful for the researcher. There are numerous templates available for researchers to create their own research log[3] and they can customize the research log how they see fit. Information about sources, including citations and quotes, can be copied from premium legal databases. Basic elements that should be a part of each research log include:

- Citation of the resource;

- Search terms used to locate the resource;

- Location of the resource (Lexis, Westlaw, internet, print);

- Summary/value/findings of the resource;

- Date accessed; and

- Status/validity of the resource (overruled on other grounds, distinguished, criticized, last updated).

---

3. Lintz, *supra* note 2; Osborne, *supra* note 1, at 194; *Legal Research Strategy: Research Log FAQ*, Paul L. Boley Library, Lewis & Clark Law School, library.lclark. edu/c.php?g=338750&p=3793227 [https://perma.cc/89F8-SG4F].

IV. Organizing Your Documents

Researchers benefit from systematically annotating and organizing the primary and secondary legal materials that will be useful in resolving the legal issue. Premium legal databases have simplified this process with foldering and annotation options within their systems. Researchers do not have to rely on those options, however. If the research is done on a platform without electronic folders, researchers can make folders within their computer or the cloud to capture PDFs of the legal materials that they are relying on.

Regardless of platform, researchers can use electronic folders to organize their research by client, issue, and type of material (secondary sources, statutes, cases, regulations, etc.). These folders can be further divided into subfolders that will assist researchers in quickly locating the material type they want to review (cases for/against the client, secondary sources, statutes and regulations on various topics or issues).

V. Notes on Research

In addition to organizing your research documents, it is important to take notes on the resources that will be used. These notes will assist the researcher in providing full and complete attribution to the sources cited. Also, they allow for interruption and return to a research project, minimizing wasted time. Researchers have many options for taking notes. Premium legal databases support text highlighting and the addition of notes to legal materials.

Researchers can take notes in other ways as well. These notes can be on a separate document, part of the research log, or written on the document itself, but it is necessary to take notes during the research process. Quality notes remind researchers why the documents were selected, whether the documents have been considered and rejected as irrelevant, how the researcher intends to use the document, and more. The type of material being reviewed dictates the type of notes that are recommended.

A. Secondary Sources

Researchers should provide a summary of each secondary source that proves to be substantially helpful in the research process. These summaries should contain: the citation to the resource as well as describe what was specifically useful about the resource (background, list of cases, form template, checklist of issues, etc.). Then the researcher should briefly summarize the analysis set forth in the secondary source. These summaries can simply copy and paste the relevant information from the resource, or it can be in the researcher's own words. If copied directly, include quotation marks to indicate attribution. Secondary source summaries should provide enough information so that the researcher can instantly recognize the resource and why she selected it.

B. Cases

The researcher should compile a list of cases that provides citations and a summary of why each case was selected by the researcher. The citation should include pin cites, notes that pinpoint the pages within the cited source that are relevant or quoted, where appropriate so the researcher can quickly locate the relevant portion of a case. The summary does not need to be a full brief of the case, but it should provide at least the holding and reasoning of the case, and how it applies to the matter at hand.

If a case has a warning citator signal or has been validated, notes about the validity of the case should be included as well.

C. Statutes

The researcher should include the citation to, a summary of, or the text of each statutory section that is critical to the legal issues. There could be multiple statutory sections that effect the legal issues because the elements, definitions, procedural matters, exceptions, penalties, and other provisions may be located throughout different sections. Researchers need to provide a citation to each relevant statutory section. Any negative citator treatment should also be noted. If the legal issue involves an act that took place some time ago, researchers should note when the statute was enacted or last amended.

VI. Ending Your Research

One of the most difficult problems in legal research is knowing when to stop. Certainly, time and cost deadlines may decide this for researchers, but researchers also need to know when it is time to stop researching and begin writing.

The key thing for researchers to recognize is that many legal issues will not have clear answers. There will be some legal issues that have definite answers, but many times researchers will need to carefully analyze the existing law to predict the likely outcome of a legal issue based on the facts.

If researchers encounter a legal issue that does not seem to have a definitive answer, this is where the research plan can offer a substantial benefit. Researchers need to review their research plan in connection with their research so far and determine whether every applicable term has been used and whether there are any other primary and secondary sources that need to be consulted. Researchers may need to refine their approach after they review their research results in consultation with the research plan. These different approaches may include using other terms, synonyms, broadening the issue, using citators to locate additional materials, or utilizing different legal databases or resources. Researchers can essentially use the research plan as a checklist that they have done everything possible during the legal research process.

As a practical matter, if different approaches all lead to the same primary and secondary materials, then researchers can be confident that they have reviewed all of the on point primary and secondary materials. There are no guarantees in legal research, but if you follow the suggestions set forth in Chapter 1 and in this chapter, researchers can feel assured they have done everything necessary to locate the applicable primary law to apply to their factual scenario.

VII. Organizing Your Analysis

Once it is determined that the research is complete, it is time to organize your analysis of the legal issue(s). The summaries of primary and secondary materials will be very helpful. Researchers can develop an outline to assist them in organizing their legal analysis. This outline can be organized by legal issue. This outline will allow researchers to provide the synthesized legal rule from relevant primary materials, list helpful secondary sources explaining the rule, and provide a list of primary materials that specifically apply the legal rule to the facts subject to the research. A sample analysis chart is set forth in Table 2-2.

Table 2-2. Sample Analysis Chart

Legal Issue: Under Georgia law, after receiving a request from a shareholder, does a private corporation have to provide the shareholder with a third-party appraisal of the corporation that was done at the request of the board of directors?

Controlling Statute: O.C.G.A. § 14-1602(c) "A shareholder of a corporation is entitled to inspect and copy … [the] [a]ccounting records of the corporation"
 (d) A shareholder may inspect and copy the records described in subsection (c) of this Code section only if:
     (1) His demand is made in good faith and for a proper purpose that is reasonably relevant to his legitimate interest as a shareholder;
     (2) He describes with reasonable particularity his purpose and the records he desires to inspect;
     (3) The records are directly connected with his purpose; and
     (4) The records are to be used only for the stated purpose.

Case	Summary	Application
Riser v. Genuine Parts Co., 150 Ga. App. 502, 504, (1979).	Shareholders' right to corporate records does not "extend automatically to the obtention of income tax returns, and general demands which are overly broad in their scope."	Shareholders' rights to corporate records is not absolute.
G.I.R. Sys., Inc. v. Lance, 219 Ga. App. 829, 831 (1995).	Private corporation must disclose records available through an audit engagement so that a shareholder may value the stock.	If the shareholder has a legitimate reason for disclosure of documents, a corporation may need to provide documents produced by a third-party.
Master Mortg. Corp. v. Craven, 127 Ga. App. 367, 371 (1972).	Stockholder was not entitled to the inspection of "tax returns, and especially the worksheets used in their preparation."	Corporation may restrict access to underlying documents.

VIII. Conclusion

Research plans and logs are essential elements of the research process. These will make the research more efficient and provide documentation of the research. Once the research is complete, researchers can organize their analysis based on the notes they compiled during the research process.

Appendix 2-1.

SAMPLE COMPLETED RESEARCH PLAN

Relevant Facts:

Leia was driving through downtown Atlanta. Unknown to her, a Dragon-Con event was occurring. While stopped at a red light, she became nervous, because she noticed large crowds gathering on the sidewalks. A group of costumed aliens and monsters then swarmed across the road in front of her. Due to the costumes' realistic and frightening nature, her children began to scream. As a result, Leia accelerated, ran through the red light, and injured Luke S., a bystander on the crosswalk not involved in the parade. His leg was crushed and required surgery. He has sued Leia for his injuries.

Issue(s):

Under Georgia law, what is the liability for a vehicle driver who, while running a red light, strikes a pedestrian on the crosswalk? Are there potential defenses based on the driver's state of mind/fear? Does the fact that she was genuinely frightened for not only her own but her children's well-being relieve her liability?

Jurisdiction:

Georgia – State Law

Search Terms:

driver, motorist, pedestrian, crowd, parade, red light, sidewalk, pedestrian injury, intersection, right of way, crowd, children, distraction, fear, panic, danger, injury, liability, exception, defense, negligence, duty of care, emergency, right of way, injury, tort, emergency rule, conduct in emergency situations

Potential Sources:

Georgia Jurisprudence on motor vehicle defenses

Georgia treatise on tort law and defenses

Treatises on motor vehicle negligence, prefer Georgia focus

Georgia statutes on duties of drivers of motor vehicle/exceptions

Georgia cases involving panic or emergency by driver

Misc.:

Due date is September 24 at 5:00 pm. Time frame for assignment is 3–4 hours. Client request is to identify possible defense(s) for her negligent collision with Luke. Focus on claims against Leia, another associate is looking at the claims and issues against the city, county, or state government.

Chapter 3

Research Techniques

After reading this chapter, you will be able to:

- Consider the cost and accessibility of legal research sources when choosing sources;

- Evaluate sources based on legal information literacy criteria including authority, weight, currentness, relevance, completeness and efficiency; and

- Apply research techniques to locate relevant legal information in a source, such as

  - Browse or search;

  - Mine/Evaluate; and

  - Help tools.

Researchers generally begin their legal research online, though print resources and tools remain important for a variety of reasons. In this chapter, we will consider the role that cost and accessibility of legal research sources play in determining the research path. We will review considerations of basic legal information literacy to evaluate sources. The considerations include authority, weight, currentness, relevance, completeness, and efficiency. Finally, we will consider a variety of techniques routinely used by researchers and librarians to locate relevant legal information in a source.

I. Choosing Sources

The first step of choosing sources is looking in the right place, like looking for statutes in the statutory code rather than the compiled regulations. However, there are many sources for statutes, and this section guides us to choose among the many sources that might contain the needed legal information. Primary considerations include cost, accessibility, and those related to legal information literacy.

A. Cost

Primary sources, the laws themselves, are generally freely available online. Although we don't all have easy access to the web at home, access is available through public libraries and law libraries, including county law libraries. Using search engines, researchers can find statutes, regulations, and cases in their jurisdictions from free sources such as state legislatures, agencies, and courts. Official sources may be available for free, though they may not include any extra tools that will help you to use them more effectively. Table 3-1 includes a list of recommended free online sources for Georgia legal materials.

It can be harder to locate secondary sources, such as treatises that explain the law, freely on the web. However, there are other sources such as journal articles, blog posts, and other web posts, that may explain the law in an easy-to-understand way. Additionally, the *Official Code of Georgia*, including its annotations has been available freely online since March 2022.

Some researchers pay to use premium databases to conduct legal research. The costs associated with using the premium tools may be worth it to the researcher. The premium databases providers, like Lexis and Westlaw, often are also publishers for the specialized treatises in the law, and their databases include access to those helpful secondary sources. Also, the editorial content that the premium database providers add to the law, such as case annotations for statutes or regulations, makes research easier and simplifies the process of updating the law.

Costs associated with using premium databases, particularly Lexis and Westlaw, may be controlled by application of some of the search strategies and techniques described below. To assure that you are maximizing your cost efficiency as you use the databases, you should consult with database training materials and representatives.

Table 3-1. Free Sources for Georgia Primary Materials

Type of Legal Material	Official Free Source	URL
Official Code of Georgia (O.C.G.A.)	Georgia Legislature site	www.lexisnexis.com/hottopics/gacode/default.asp
Georgia regulations	Official compilation of regulations	https://rules.sos.ga.gov/Home.aspx
Attorney General opinions	Attorney General site	law.georgia.gov/opinions
GA Supreme court opinions	Supreme Court of Georgia	Gasupreme.us
Georgia Court of Appeals opinions	Court of Appeals of Georgia	Gaappeals.us

B. Evaluating Resources of Legal Information

Before relying upon legal information sources, researchers need to evaluate the sources according to some basic criteria that help assure that the information is reliable and valid. The points of evaluation are authority, weight, currentness, relevance, and completeness. Official sources of law are generally assumed to be reliable, and their validity is assessed using a citator, as described in Chapter 11. The following description of criteria should be applied in evaluating secondary sources, or those which describe and explain the law, and unofficial primary sources.

i. Authority

When considering a source of legal information, the authority of the source is a key point. Secondary sources explain the law and provide citations to primary sources of the law, so a knowledgeable and trustworthy source is helpful. In these contexts, it is helpful to consider the author or publisher. Is the author or publisher clearly indicated, and apparently knowledgeable in the area? When evaluating a free website, does it have a reputation for reliability, as does the Cornell Legal Information Institute? Or is it unknown? Does the author or publisher have a motivation or apparent agenda that would affect the accuracy of the description of the law?

ii. Weight

Sources of law have different weights. The Constitution is the source of authority for all other law, and thus it has the most weight. Statutes carry more weight than regulations. Cases interpret statutes, and thus may not be as weighty or helpful as statutes. An exception to that guideline is when an area of law is developed only through caselaw, also called common law, and there are no statutes.

A second consideration when determining the weight of a source of law is whether the source is the law of the jurisdiction. The law of the relevant jurisdiction is mandatory law, while the laws of other jurisdictions are only persuasive. In a Georgia-based legal problem, the law of Georgia would carry weight, while the laws of another jurisdiction would be merely persuasive.

Secondary sources are evaluated differently than primary sources. Researchers often consult secondary sources for an explanation of the law and citations to the law. Some secondary sources are national in scope, while others may be limited to specific jurisdictions. And courts generally consider very few, if any, secondary sources to be weighty authorities. However, secondary sources should not be discarded from consideration just because they are national in scope. They remain helpful to researchers for their explanation of the law and their citations to primary sources, so long as the researcher evaluates the contents with jurisdiction in mind.

iii. Currentness

Legislatures, executive leaders, agencies, and courts are all capable of taking action to make or change existing laws at any time. Because laws are always subject to change, researchers must make sure to evaluate whether the laws are current, as discussed in Chapter 11 about citators.

Similar considerations arise in evaluating secondary sources and unofficial sources of primary law. Is the source current? When was the last time the source was updated? Do you know whether there have been changes since the source was last updated?

In Georgia, the legislative session normally lasts 40 legislative days, with the last legislative day typically in late March or early April.[1] Therefore, unless

---

1. Ballotpedia provides a listing of the start and end days for the Georgia legislative sessions since 2010. *See Georgia General Assembly*, Ballotpedia, https://ballotpedia.org/Georgia_General_Assembly [https://perma.cc/2A2E-97T4].

a special legislative session is called, a source for statutes that is updated in June will likely reflect the current law, while a source that was last updated in February or March may not reflect the current law.

iv. Relevance

An obvious consideration for researchers is relevance. It is easy to see, for example, when researching about how to handle the probate of your grandmother's estate that you would not need to consult primary or secondary sources about criminal procedure in Georgia. However, when evaluating results in a resource that is only about probate of an estate, such as Professor Mary Radford's *Redfearn Wills and Administration in Georgia*, it may be harder to figure out which part of the treatise is helpful. Keeping in mind your research question when using the source will be addressed more in Part II of this chapter.

v. Completeness

Completeness has a few considerations. The question of completeness initially is straightforward: Does this resource have all the information it should have in it? For example, agency websites often include regulations that are relevant, such as the Georgia State Board of Worker's Compensation.[2] However, a researcher may need to consult a general rule outside the scope of the agency rules, and it may not be included on their site. For example, federal regulations may be relevant, as might those of other Georgia agencies. A researcher would need to consult other sources for a complete search in that instance.

Researchers may also describe a source as complete based on the scope and depth of coverage. In the online context, researchers often prefer premium database providers such as Fastcase, Lexis, and Westlaw because they include statutes, regulations, cases, and executive actions from both federal and state governments. Also, the availability of secondary sources that link a researcher quickly from one source to anther improves research efficiency.

---

2. *Rules*, State Board of Worker's Compensation, https://sbwc.georgia.gov/statutes-and-rules/rules [https://perma.cc/FV5K-B8KN].

Figure 3-1. Georgia Legislative Documents Help Menu[3]

Server S|A GALILEO Digital Initiative Database
While in this database, use the Search button below.

Georgia Legislative Documents   Search

Help Menu

- The Georgia Legislative Documents provide access to three legislative resources:
  - Acts of the General Assembly of the state of Georgia
  - Journal of the House of Representatives of the State of Georgia
  - Journal of the Senate of the State of Georgia

  The Acts are the actual text of the laws and resolutions as they were voted upon by the General Assembly. The text as published in the Acts is different from the text published in the Georgia Code. The Acts to be included in the database were published 1774-1995.

  The Journals outline the passage of bills and resolutions through each chamber of the General Assembly. The House of Representatives Journals to be included in the database were published 1781-1995; the Senate Journals to be included were published 1789-1995.

- Searching Tips
- Displaying Search Results
- How to override default truncation search (e.g., search *complete* words only)

  NOTE: When viewing full text, use the browser's **Find** feature to search for occurrences of words.

Online databases usually indicate information about the database, such as the scope of information included. It may indicate that the database contains information, such as statutes, only going back to a particular date in time. The Georgia Legislative Documents database is an example of one which has helpful scope information. Figure 3.1 shows that the acts included in the database range from 1774 to 1995, but do not include current legislative documents. Some databases may look complete, but the results retrieved may not include tables, charts, or other illustrations that would exist in the original print documents.

Although it is often easier to start in online resources, it may be the case that print resources are more complete. Not every secondary source related to Georgia law is available online, which means that an evaluation of completeness may end with the conclusion that the researcher needs to check a print source.

3. *Georgia Legislative Documents: Help Menu*, GALILEO Digital Initiatives Database, http://neptune3.galib.uga.edu/ssp/cgi-bin/ftaccess.cgi?location=fhtml/legis/help.html&hfrom=fhtml/legis/simple.html&sessionid=7f000001 [https://perma.cc/MC5Z-JDNJ]. Image used with permission.

vi. Efficiency

A final consideration for researchers is whether the resource being evaluated is the most efficient one to use to research a problem. Sometimes, the work required to learn how to use an online source outweighs the simplicity and ease of consulting the print equivalent of the source. Researchers may also consider the cost of a resource in evaluating its efficiency. Costs may include purchasing a treatise outright, which can be quite expensive. But other costs may include finding web access, paying for a subscription to a premium database, and others.

II. Researcher Techniques

Researchers use a variety of techniques or strategies to efficiently use legal resources. These techniques work most effectively when the researcher has already identified the legal issue being researched. This section will address searching and browsing strategies as well as mining resources and narrowing a results list.

A. Browsing

Browsing is one of the most common strategies researchers use to explore resources. Browsers start at the title level of a resource and focus downward, typically by skimming a table of contents. Law materials may include both an abbreviated and an extended table of contents, which helps researchers browse more efficiently. They may identify the chapter of interest in the abbreviated table of contents and then turn to the extended table of contents to identify the section(s) within that chapter that are of particular interest for the research question.

To browse effectively, it helps for the researcher to have a research question in mind. That way, the researcher can easily evaluate whether the source is helpful or relevant to answer the research question. Browsing works effectively both online and in print.

Browsing can be a process of trial and error, as potentially helpful avenues are investigated and later disregarded. Researchers often say, however, that even false starts down the wrong path give them more context for their questions and are not a waste of time. When you find a helpful entry in a secondary source or statute or regulation, a key practice is to "check the neighborhood." Legal resources, particularly primary sources that are codified or secondary sources that are divided into sections, are organized so that information on the same topic can be found together, in a "neighborhood" made of nearby sections. A definition that helps the researcher understand a substantive statute is found nearby the substantive statute, for example.

B. Searching

Starting with a legal issue in mind, searching in print is most efficiently done by using print indexes. Though online searchers may also use indexes when researching, they more often do simple keyword or advanced searching of documents.

i. Indexes

When using indexes, the researcher identifies a significant word or concept that may be relevant and checks the index for that word, reviewing the places within the legal research resource that are suggested as helpful. Researching using an index is a process of elimination, reviewing each of the suggested parts of the source to evaluate whether any are helpful.

Sometimes an index includes a "See" reference, or a "See also" reference. A "See" reference is used to indicate that the term being searched is not the proper term, such as when a researcher looks for an acronym and is referred to see the index for the spelled-out words for the acronym. A "See also" reference is an indication that a researcher who is interested in a particular topic may want to see also a related topic.

Sometimes an index is found at the end of a book that is a single volume. Other times, an index may be a multi-volume set at the end of a much larger set. The level of detail available in an index varies from resource to resource. Some indexes are brief, while others are quite deep. Some online resources also contain indexes. Online indexes function in the same way as print indexes. Indexes are useful whether they are used in print or online.

ii. Simple or Keyword Searching

Researchers using online resources are more likely to engage in keyword searching, though some premium databases include tables of contents and indexes for specific titles, such as treatises or statutes. We are familiar with the idea of simple or keyword searching because we are familiar with using search engines such as Google, Yahoo, Bing, and DuckDuckGo to search the web. We expect that a Google search, for example, will include the words searched in the results list.

Some researchers using these search engines type a question directly into the search box, while others include only meaningful terms related to the search. Search engines are designed to locate relevant information based on the search query. Behind the scenes, search engines apply proprietary algorithms, or rules, to your search query to make your search as effective as possible.

Premium legal research database providers, such as Fastcase, Lexis, and Westlaw, each use their own algorithms when a researcher runs as a simple or keyword search. In legal searching, an *algorithm* is the rules or instructions that the database search engines are programmed to follow when a researcher enters a search query. In a premium legal research database, algorithms may add legal terms of art or other synonyms to a researcher's simple search, based on the terms used by the researcher. For example, a researcher may use the search term child, but the algorithm may also add minor and infant as additional terms.

When running a basic search in a database, the search should include words or concepts that the researcher thinks may be included in the type of document that the researcher needs. These may include types of parties, legally significant facts, or possible claims or defenses. Simple or keyword searching is recommended for novice searchers, particularly if the researcher is learning a new area of law.

iii. Advanced Searching

Researchers may choose instead to run an advanced search, whether they are using search engines like Google or premium legal research database providers. When selecting an advanced search, the researcher may have more control over the search. Advanced search tools may allow the researcher to require that particular words appear in a certain proximity, such as in the same sentence or only in the same document, or to require that words appear in certain places, such as particular parts of a document.

Premium legal research database providers offer instructions as to how to use their services. Those instructions are one of the most valuable tools for a researcher who wants to run an advanced search. Because the research providers have different owners in addition to their own proprietary algorithms, there is no guarantee that the rules that work for advanced searching on one provider's platform will work on another's platform.

Another advantage of advanced searching is that you may be able to search particular parts of a document for information, instead of searching an entire document. For example, you may want to look for words that appear in the title of a document because the word appearing in the title is a good indicator that the document would be mostly about that word. A document that only had that word in a single paragraph would be less likely to be helpful.

The type of information being searched presents an important consideration in search development. A researcher should use different terms and connectors when building an advanced search in a database that includes only citation information for journal articles as compared with searching in a database containing the citation information and also full text of the accompanying articles. If only titles are being searched, a connector requiring terms to be in the same paragraph is not meaningful, for example.

A related consideration relates to the specificity of terms used in a search. Long documents, such as multi-volume treatises, may treat a subject with greater depth and use more terms of art or more specific search terms, as compared with shorter documents such as cases or statutes. Similarly, the number of concepts required in a search may be smaller in shorter documents, such as statutes, and larger in longer documents, such as treatises or cases.

When building an advanced search, there are a few principles to keep in mind.

1. The more terms that are required in the search, the narrower the search results.
2. You may need to supply synonyms for terms to be as inclusive as you mean to be.
3. Use the terms and connectors provided by the legal research service.
4. Consider searching specific document parts if it is helpful.
5. Select a jurisdictional focus for your search in advance or by filtering results, rather than by including the jurisdiction as a search term.

Advanced searching is often done in combination with simple or keyword searching. A researcher may begin with a simple keyword search and then, in the next iteration of the search, may switch to an advanced search.

iv. Evaluating Search Results

Whether you ran a simple search or an advanced search, the steps involved in evaluating the results are the same. When you review and evaluate search results, you need to have your legal research question in mind. You can compare the results with the legal research question to analyze whether the results are relevant or helpful in answering your question.

As you make that comparison, you will want to understand how the results are displayed. Search results may be displayed in a variety of ways. Results may be displayed by relevance (typically determined by the algorithms of the database provider), date, alphabetical order, etc. You may be able to navigate and review the results more efficiently if you understand how the results are ordered. Many databases allow researchers to rearrange results according to preference.

You will want to take notes on relevant results that you identify in case you need to apply any other research strategies, such as checking the "neighborhood," to expand your search further.

C. Mining a Source

When you have identified a useful source, whether because somebody suggested it at the start of your research or because you browsed or searched effectively, you may want to mine the source to expand your search. You may be expanding your search to find additional information, or you may be expanding your search to find information that is more helpful. You may mine secondary sources and primary sources. *Mining* refers to identifying cited sources, such as those found listed in footnotes, and consulting them to expand your research.

We often think of mining secondary source footnotes. The footnotes to secondary sources often contain citations to the primary sources that are being described. They may also contain citations to secondary sources that are also relevant to the topic.

Some primary sources may be mined also. Cases, for example, contain many citations to primary sources that may be helpful to a researcher such as statutes and regulations. They also sometimes have footnotes that may cite to secondary sources as well as primary sources that are relevant to the legal issue. Other primary sources may provide citation information that can be used to locate additional related information, such as consulting the history of a statute to identify citations that will help the researcher find legislative history information for the statute.

Of course, once a source has been mined, the citations identified need to be evaluated with the legal research question in mind. Citations found by mining sources can be especially valuable because the context for the citation helps the researcher tell whether the source is likely to be helpful.

D. Narrowing Results

Another helpful approach to research involves narrowing the results to identify helpful sources. Narrowing results is a useful strategy because it makes the number of results that need to be reviewed smaller, allowing the researcher to focus on results that are more likely to be helpful. For example, a researcher investigating the application of a statute that was passed in 2015 may consider narrowing results of a search to include only results published in 2015 or later.

Results from premium legal research database providers are often narrowed by date, as in the example above. They may also be narrowed by the resource type (type of secondary or primary source), jurisdiction, or words contained within the source. A researcher may narrow a single search by multiple criteria, or facets. Some search sources offer the researcher the opportunity to narrow the search before running the search, as well.

E. Seek Help

Whether beginning your research, or stumped midway through your research plan, researchers are encouraged to seek help. Law librarians are specially trained to assist legal researchers who have varying familiarity with the law. Law libraries often have information about reference services, including reference by chat, email, and telephone. You may find law librarians at court or county law libraries and academic law libraries in Georgia.

In addition to law librarians, many online research tools include help or Frequently Asked Question (FAQ) sections on their sites. Some also include chat or telephone assistance. Take advantage of the resources provided by legal database providers. Their help can make your research go more smoothly.

III. Conclusion

Researchers make a variety of judgments as they research an area of law. In addition to considerations related to information literacy, such as the authority, weight, relevance, currentness, and completeness of a source, researchers also consider the best ways that sources may be used to further the research agenda. Sometimes a researcher will browse a source, but other times the researcher may need to use either basic or advanced (terms and connectors) searches. Regardless of those choices, the researcher is consistently evaluating whether the information identified is responsive to the researcher's needs or raises additional questions. Asking law librarians for assistance when researching is a valuable strategy that can help focus research and save researcher time.

Chapter 4

Secondary Sources

After reading this chapter you will be able to:

- Explain the value of using secondary sources in legal research;
- Differentiate between the different types of secondary sources; and
- Recognize where to find secondary sources.

This chapter defines secondary sources, explains why to use secondary sources in legal research, and then describes different types of secondary sources. A secondary source contains information written *about* the law, compared to primary materials, which *are* the law. Primary materials are the laws created by the various branches of government, which include statutes, cases, and administrative materials. Primary sources bind a court of that jurisdiction, while secondary sources are not binding on a court unless they have been adopted by the jurisdiction. Secondary sources help individuals understand the law or help them perform the various legal activities that legal professionals encounter.

I. Benefits of Secondary Sources

There are several benefits to using secondary sources as part of the legal research process which are discussed below.

A. Efficiency

A legal researcher can be much more efficient by using secondary sources because the research has already been performed. Secondary sources include analysis and citation of the relevant law, and researchers can use the research and analysis set forth in the various types of secondary materials to assist them in resolving the legal issue(s). Researchers will be much more efficient by consulting a secondary source's research and analysis, rather than doing that same research and analysis themselves.

B. Background Information

Secondary sources provide researchers with the essential background information they need to move forward in the legal research process. Researchers often encounter new areas of law that they are unfamiliar with. It is difficult, if not impossible, to identify the relevant legal issues or conduct effective searches, when the researcher does not have a basic foundation of the legal topic. Secondary sources can provide researchers with the terminology of the legal topic and give them an understanding of the various issues involved. This foundation will permit researchers to create efficient searches and identity potential legal issues.

C. Primary Sources

Secondary sources refer the researcher to relevant primary sources on a legal topic. The authors of the secondary sources have researched the legal topic or issue, identified relevant cases, statutes, administrative materials, and have provided summaries and explanations. The researcher can use these primary sources to locate additional secondary and primary sources by consulting a citator as discussed in Chapter 11.

D. Forms

There are a variety of forms available for both litigation and transactional matters within secondary sources. These are valuable to attorneys because they may be drafted in light of existing law, and they save the attorney and client valuable time compared to drafting basic forms from scratch. Forms include sample complaints, motions, contracts, estate planning documents, and other types of forms. Secondary sources provide attorneys with a template that they can customize for the specific matter that they are dealing with. Forms may be found in treatises, practice materials, topical services, form books, and continuing legal education materials.

There are other sources that researchers can consult for form templates as well. The State Courts of Georgia provide freely accessible forms on a variety of matters on its website.[1] Some of the Georgia county court websites also provide freely accessible forms. Researchers will need to browse the various court websites to determine which forms are available and locate forms appropriate to a specific court. Some examples of court websites providing forms are set forth in Table 4-1.

Table 4-1. Forms

County	Web Address
Cobb County Court Forms	www.cobbcounty.org/courts/law-library (navigate to the Self-Help Center)
Dougherty County Forms	www.dougherty.ga.us/public-safety/public-resources/law-library/find-a-form
Forsyth County Court Forms	forsythcourts.com/Resources/Law-Library

Researchers can also find statutory forms in the Official Code of Georgia Annotated (O.C.G.A.). Statutory forms may be found online by searching for the name of the form and the jurisdiction.

E. Checklists

Checklists are one of the best tools for attorneys. Whether your focus is on litigation or transactional matters, checklists can ensure that nothing essential has been missed. These can be used to identify claims and defenses, organize a business entity, assist in closing a transaction, drafting a contract, and assist in all kinds of legal transactional and litigation matters. Forms, treatises, practice materials, topical services, and continuing legal education materials provide researchers with sample checklists that they can customize for their specific purposes.

F. Persuasive Authority

Sometimes there is not a mandatory primary material on point for the relevant legal issue. When this occurs, researchers may use secondary sources as persuasive authority. Researchers can provide citations to secondary

---

1. Council of State Court Judges of Georgia, *State Court Forms* (2021), georgia-courts.gov/statecourt/state-court-behind-the-bench/state-court-forms [https://perma.cc/JH86-Q9FX].

sources that support their position on the legal issue. The court is not obligated to follow the assertions set forth in a secondary source, but resources such as restatements and model laws, described more below, and those by notable authors are highly respected by the courts and may be persuasive to judges.

G. Refocusing

Researchers may become lost or confused during the legal research process. Researchers may not fully understand the legal topic or the relevant primary materials. They may find themselves going down rabbit-holes that are not appropriate to the applicable legal issue(s). Secondary sources are a great way to get researchers back on the correct path or clarify confusing legal topics and primary materials.

II. Types of Secondary Materials

There are several types of secondary sources available to assist with legal research. These include legal encyclopedias, practice materials, treatises, *American Law Reports*, legal periodicals, and Restatements of the Law. The type of secondary source used by a researcher will differ depending on what the researcher is trying to accomplish. You can determine which type of resource(s) will be suitable for a specific research project based on that source's attributes.

A. Legal Encyclopedias

Legal encyclopedias are a great starting place for researchers who encounter a new legal topic, need a brief introduction to a topic, or need a quick answer to a legal issue. As the name suggests, legal encyclopedias span a large variety of topics but do not go into much detail. They can be used by researchers to locate answers to a general legal issue, obtain initial search terms, or find references to basic primary law materials so they can expand their research. Researchers focusing on Georgia law and electing to use a legal encyclopedia to start their research should begin with *Georgia Jurisprudence*.

1. Georgia Jurisprudence

Georgia Jurisprudence, a West publication, contains analysis on a variety of legal topics based on the cases, statutes, and administrative law of Georgia. *Georgia Jurisprudence* is not arranged alphabetically by topic. The volumes are organized by topic and then divided into sub-topics. The topics are listed in Table 4-2.

Table 4-2. *Georgia Jurisprudence* Volumes

Property (Vols. 1–3A)	Decedent's Estates and Trusts (Vols. 10–11)
Business and Commercial Law: Business Torts and Trade Regulation (Vol. 4)	Workers' Compensation (Vol. 12)
Business and Commercial Law: Uniform Commercial Code (Vol. 5 and Vol. 5A)	Personal Injury Torts (Vols. 13–15)
Business and Commercial Law: Corporations, Other Business Organizations and Securities Regulation (Vol. 6)	Insurance (Vol. 16 and 16A)
Business and Commercial Law: Contracts (Vol. 7)	Employment and Labor (Vol. 17)
Family Law (Vol. 8)	Criminal Law (Vols. 18–20)
Environmental Law (Vol. 9)	

Georgia Jurisprudence is available in print and on Westlaw. In the print version, there is an index to help locate applicable sections, a Table of Cases, and a Table of Statutes and Rules, all of which are updated annually. These tables permit researchers to locate sections citing to a specific Georgia or federal case, statute, or rule they are researching. Encyclopedia entries include references to other secondary sources published by West.

If a researcher would like to use a legal encyclopedia to get an overview of her topic and it is not analyzed in *Georgia Jurisprudence* or is not discussed thoroughly, the researcher may consult one, or both, of the national legal encyclopedias discussed below.

2. American Jurisprudence

American Jurisprudence, Second Edition (Am.Jur.2d), is one of these nationally based legal encyclopedias. This publication by West analyzes both state and federal law on over 400 topics. Am.Jur.2d is organized alphabetically by topic and provides analysis to broad legal principles commonly encountered by attorneys. This resource is available in print, on Lexis, and on Westlaw. It contains more analysis of federal statutory materials than C.J.S., discussed below. It also includes references to relevant West topics and key numbers, secondary sources published by West, and citations to primary materials from jurisdictions throughout the United States.

3. Corpus Juris Secondum

Corpus Juris Secondum (C.J.S.) is the other legal encyclopedia with a national scope. This is also published by West and is very similar to Am.Jur.2d. However, there are a couple of differences. First, C.J.S. tends to focus on case law rather than statutory law, and it also contains more citations to primary materials. Unlike Am.Jr.2d, this resource is only available in print and on Westlaw; it is not available in Lexis. It also includes references to relevant West topics and key numbers, secondary sources published by West, and citations to primary materials.

B. Treatises and Practice Materials

Treatises and practice materials are used by researchers to gain a deeper understanding of a legal topic. Generally, treatises tend to have comprehensive coverage of a broad topic of the law. Practice materials may focus on narrow topics of the law and also provide materials on how to perform various litigation and transactional matters commonly occurring within the topic. Practice materials may include sample forms, checklists, discovery examples, procedural rules, and other items to assist legal professionals.

Georgia treatises and practice materials are an excellent place for Georgia researchers to start their research, and a list of these resources is included in Appendix B. Practical Guidance in Lexis and Practical Law in Westlaw are also great resources for Georgia practice materials. These databases contain Practice Notes, which are summaries of the law on various topics, and provide Georgia specific forms, clauses, and checklists. Researchers can browse by topic within these databases or conduct searches to locate relevant materials.

If researchers want to locate additional treatises and practice materials, they can use treatise finders developed by various law libraries. [2] These guides provide lists of treatises and practice materials on different legal topics, identify which resources are considered preeminent by legal practitioners, and indicate where they are located.

Treatises and practice materials are in Fastcase, Lexis, Westlaw, and other premium legal databases. To locate a specific treatise or practice guide in Lexis and Westlaw, researchers can select secondary sources, texts & treatises, and then browse by topic or jurisdiction. Researchers have the option to browse table of contents, or to conduct searches within one or multiple resources. If researchers know the specific title of the resource, then they can simply enter the title into the search box. Researchers can also look for print versions of these resources in a Georgia law library's catalog, but please note that some of these print titles may not be updated by the law library. Researchers will need to determine the last time a treatise has been updated when using print materials.

Law libraries located in Georgia may have access to these resources in print or provide access to them online. Table 4-3 contains a list of the larger law libraries located in Georgia that are open to the public. Researchers can also search for law libraries located closer to them and then use the law libraries' catalogs to determine if an applicable title is available in print or online through the law library.

---

2. *Treatises by Topic*, Georgia State University College of Law Library, https://libguides.law.gsu.edu/TreatisesByTopic [https://perma.cc/G6RV-4PDH]; *Treatise Finders*, Georgetown Law Library, guides.ll.georgetown.edu/home/treatise-finders; [https://perma.cc/TZ4U-8HKR]; Catherine Biondo, *Legal Treatise by Subject*, Harvard Law Library, guides.library.harvard.edu/legaltreatises [https://perma.cc/UF9V-LYZZ]; *Treatise Finder: Treatise by Subject*, University of Michigan Law Library, libguides.law.umich.edu/treatise-finder [https://perma.cc/U8N2-YWVR] are examples of treaties finders.

Table 4-3. Law Libraries in Georgia

Law Library Name	Web Site
Cobb County Law Library	www.cobbcounty.org/courts/law-library
Dekalb County Superior Court Law Library	www.dekalbsuperiorcourt.com/law-library/about-the-law-library/
Fulton County Superior Court Law Library	www.fultoncourt.org/library/
Georgia State University College of Law Library	lawlibrary.gsu.edu/
Homer M. Stark Law Library (Gwinnett County)	www.gcll.org/about.html
Mercer University Furman Smith Law Library	law.mercer.edu/library/
Augusta-Richmond County Law Library	www.augustaga.gov/1992/Law-Library
University of Georgia Law Library	www.law.uga.edu/law-library

C. Continuing Legal Education Materials

Continuing legal education materials (CLEs) are another good practice material for both novice and experienced attorneys. Every lawyer licensed in Georgia is required to complete CLE courses periodically to maintain their license. These courses are targeted to attorneys that want to learn about a new legal topic or to attorneys that want to obtain advanced skills in a legal area. These courses are presented by experienced attorneys, judges, and law professors. As part of these courses, the presenters will provide explanations, analysis, forms, and checklists.

While there are many organizations that produce CLEs, the Institute of Continuing Legal of Education of Georgia focuses on creating CLEs for Georgia attorneys. These materials may be available for purchase at the ICLE website[3] and some may also be found at the Georgia law libraries listed above by using the libraries' catalogs.

---

3. *ICLE Programs*, State Bar of Georgia, gabar.org/membership/cle/courseschedule.cfm [https://perma.cc/TN2X-N2RU].

CLEs can also be found in Fastcase, Lexis and Westlaw. Fastcase has some CLE materials from state bar organizations. Lexis includes American Bar Association and American Law Institute publications and has more state bar associations' CLE materials. Westlaw also contains CLE materials from a variety of sources including the American Bar Association (ABA), the American Law Institute (ALI), and various state and local bar associations.

D. Topical Services

Topical services, sometimes referred to as loose-leaf services, provide the most in-depth discussion and compilation of primary materials on a particular area of the law. These are usually multi-volume treatises that contain explanations and the text of relevant statutes and regulations. They also include summaries of court and administrative decisions affecting the legal topic.

A point of value for topical services is the frequency with which they are updated. Some services may be updated in print as frequently as every week. These services are published in loose-leaf binders, with pages easily removed and replaced as the law and its explanation are updated.

Topical services seek to compile all of the relevant materials on legal topics so that researchers can find what they need in a single comprehensive tool. These materials center on legal topics that are highly regulated, such as tax, securities, employment, and environmental law. Example titles include the Standard Tax Reporter (CCH), the Employment Law Coordinator (West), and the Occupational Safety Guide (Bloomberg).

At this point, most topical services are also available online through the various publishers' online platforms and may not be available in print. Georgia law libraries are unlikely to keep these types of print materials up to date if also maintaining online access, so when reviewing print topical services in a law library, be sure to check when it was last updated.

E. Hornbooks and Nutshells

Hornbooks are a subset of treatises defined as a "book explaining the basics of a given subject."[4] Hornbooks are usually a one volume monograph written about a specific legal topic. These are primarily written for law

---

4. Hornbook, *Black's Law Dictionary* (11th ed. 2019).

students, but they can also assist researchers in understanding the basic foundations of a legal topic.

Almost every major legal topic has an applicable hornbook associated with it. These hornbooks will provide an explanation of the law and contain citations to basic primary materials as well. Researchers can find hornbooks by searching a law library's online catalog for a topic and the word hornbook. Hornbooks are not found in Lexis or Westlaw, but many law libraries will have these resources available in print.

Researchers may also encounter resources called *nutshells*. These books are essentially a condensed version of a hornbook. However, nutshells have very few citations to primary sources. These are published by West and provide an overview of the black letter law on a legal topic, often in plain language. These are written to assist law students in preparing for class or an exam, but they can also be useful to researchers trying to understand a new area of law.

F. American Law Reports

American Law Reports (ALR) are a valuable secondary source for case law research. This secondary source published by West began in the late 1800's and continues to be an important resource for researchers. Each entry in the ALR is organized around a legal issue in a case that is "reported" and includes significant commentary and analysis.

The commentary and analysis are known collectively as *annotations*. An annotation first begins with an article outline that provides a scope of the annotation, an overview of the law, and practice pointers. The annotation will then go on to summarize relevant cases throughout the United States based upon courts' holdings and the legal issues involved in the topic. At the end of an annotation there are references to other secondary materials published by West, relevant West topics and key numbers, sample search queries, and a table of statutes, cases, and rules. ALR annotations are also updated by West editors.

ALRs are not meant to be a comprehensive secondary source spanning every legal topic. The annotations in ALRs focus on specific legal issues, and on case law, but do provide some references to applicable statutes. Examples of ALR annotations include, *Liability of owner or operator of business premises for injury to patron by dog or cat; Liability of hotel or motel operator for injury or death of guest or privy resulting from condition in plumbing or bathroom of room or suite*, and *Conviction of possession of illicit drugs found in premises of which defendant was in nonexclusive possession.* Thus, you can see that these are tailored to an issue involving a specific set of facts. However, if you can locate an on-point annotation, ALRs can be extremely helpful in explaining the relevant law and locating applicable primary sources.

There are several different ALR series. One series is focused on state law (ALR, ALR 2d, ALR 3d, ALR 4th, ALR 5th, ALR 6th, and ALR 7th). The first and second series are mainly used for historical perspective at this point because they are no longer updated. Series 3d through the 7th are updated at least annually. The other series consist of annotations analyzing federal law (ALR Fed, ALR Fed 2d, and ALR Fed 3d). All of the federal series are kept up to date. Table 4-4 depicts the content of the ALR series.

Table 4-4. ALR Series

Series	Original Publication Dates	Number of Volumes
ALR	1919 to 1949	175
ALR 2d	1948 to 1965	100
ALR 3d	1965 to 1980	100
ALR 4th	1980 to 1992	90
ALR 5th	1991 to 2005	125
ALR 6th	2005 to 2015	104
ALR 7th	2015 to Present	69 as of May 2022
ALR Federal	1969 to 2005	200
ALR Federal 2d	2005 to 2015	94
ALR Federal 3d	2015 to Present	68 as of May 2022

ALRs are available in print, in Lexis, and Westlaw. If you are using the print version, there is an index for all ten of the series in a ten-volume index. West also publishes an ALR Quick Index that covers the 3d, 4th, 5th, 6th, and 7th series, which is less comprehensive than the ten-volume index. There is also a Federal ALR Quick Index that covers the federal series. The comprehensive ALR index is available in Westlaw but is not available in Lexis.

Researchers can search for relevant annotations using natural language or terms & connector searching in both of these databases.

G. Legal Periodicals

Legal periodicals, depending on their type, may offer a detailed understanding of a legal issue or present new developments in the law. There are two main types of legal periodical materials, law review articles and bar journal articles. These materials provide different types of information to researchers which will be explained below.

1. Law Review Articles

Law review articles go into detail and tend to be focused on new developments in the law. These articles are normally written by law professors or by law students. Articles written by law students are called notes or comments. However, attorneys and judges may also author law review articles. Most law review articles are published by academic law journals.

These articles can be useful in that they typically provide a background on the legal issue or topic before the author discusses the thesis. Sometimes these articles are too theoretical to be helpful for legal practitioners, so researchers may want to consult other secondary sources first. Law review articles are also not updated to include current information about the law, while many other secondary sources are updated.

While the law reviews published by the various law schools in Georgia tend to generally be based on articles national in scope, the *Georgia State University Law Review* annually dedicates its Fall issue to the Georgia General Assembly's activities and legislative intent in significant bills that were considered in that year. These are known as Peach Sheets and are further discussed in legislative history research in Chapter 10. In addition, Mercer Law Review dedicates one issue each year to developments in Georgia and Eleventh Circuit law on a variety of topics.

2. Bar Journal Articles

Bar journal articles are written specifically with practicing attorneys as the audience. These can be nationally focused, like the various American Bar Association journals, and there are also bar journals for each state, topical bar journals, and local bar journals. These types of articles are written by attorneys to provide information on new developments in the law within the relevant jurisdiction, advice on how to handle various legal matters, or an overview of a specific legal topic.

Bar journal articles are meant to provide researchers with a general overview of a legal topic and provide citations to the basic primary materials. These are helpful to gain a background on a legal topic, but researchers will most likely need to review other secondary sources as well. The State Bar of Georgia currently publishes two publications, The *Georgia Bar Journal*, which is published six times a year and is available for free online.[5] It also publishes the *YLD Review*, which is a newsletter by the Young Lawyers Division of the State Bar of Georgia. This is freely available online.[6] The Atlanta Bar Association publishes a freely accessible publication, the *Atlanta Lawyer*, which touches on a variety of topics encountered by legal professionals.[7]

3. Locating Articles

It is relatively easy to locate both law review and bar journal articles. Many of these articles can be located by searching on the internet. Google Scholar can assist researchers in focusing their results to articles published in law journals. Fastcase, Lexis, and Westlaw can also be used to locate these materials, but these databases might not have the entire set of volumes of a journal, so be sure to review the scope of coverage of a journal in a particular database. One of the best resources for law review and bar journal articles is HeinOnline, which provides PDF images of resources in its collections. Generally, HeinOnline has more complete coverage for law reviews and journals, with access to titles from the first issue to the most recent.

H. Restatements

Restatements of the Law (Restatements) are among the most authoritative secondary sources. Restatements are published by the American Law Institute (ALI). The ALI is an "organization of judges, lawyers, and law professors whose focus is to promote the clarification and simplification of the law and its better adaptation to social needs, to secure the better administration of

---

5. *Georgia Bar Journal Archives*, State Bar of Georgia, gabar.org/newsandpublications/georgiabarjournal/archive.cfm [https://perma.cc/T289-7JML].

6. *YLD Review*, State Bar of Georgia, gabar.org/newsandpublications/yldnewsletter/index.cfm [https://perma.cc/UW3L-Z8P2].

7. *Atlanta Lawyer*, Atlanta Bar Association, atlantabar.org/page/TAL [https://perma.cc/S59K-9LTD].

justice, and to encourage and carry on scholarly and scientific legal work."[8] One of ALI's endeavors is publishing the Restatements to provide clear formulation and organization of common law. The Restatements are individually published based on the topics listed in Table 4-5.

Table 4-5. *Restatement of the Law* Topics

Restatement of the Law Titles		
Agency (Third Series)	Property (Landlord and Tenant) (Second Series)	The U.S. Law of International Commercial and Investor-State Arbitration
Children and the Law	Property (Mortgages) (Third Series)	Torts: Apportionment of Liability (Third Series)
Charitable Nonprofit Organizations	Property (Servitudes) (Third Series)	Torts: Liability for Economic Harm (Third Series)
Conflict of Laws (Second) Series	Restatement of the Law Third, Property (Wills and Other Donative Transfers) (Third Series)	Torts: Intentional Torts to Persons (Third Series)
Consumer Contracts	Restitution (Third Series)	Torts: Liability for Physical and Emotional Harm (Third Series)
Contracts (Second Series)	Security & Suretyship & Guaranty (Third Series)	Torts: Products Liability (Third Series)
Employment Law	The Foreign Relations Law of the United States (Fourth Series)	Torts (Second Series)
Judgments (Second Series)	The Law Governing Lawyers (Third Series)	Trusts (Third Series)
Liability Insurance	The Law of American Indians (Third Series)	Unfair Competition (Third Series)

---

8. *How the Institute Works*, American Law Institute (2021), ali.org/about-ali/how-institute-works [https://perma.cc/9QSF-PFUU].

The table displays the most recent series for each topic. The ALI is continuing to work on the fourth series of the Restatements on Property.

Within each topic, the Restatements are organized by chapters on a major aspect of the topic. Each topic is further divided into sections which will provide a black-letter rule of law on the legal issue discussed in the section. The section will then provide comments from the drafters which explain how the rule should be interpreted, supply illustrations, and describe the development of the law. Finally, each section provides citations to cases that have cited to the rule.

Restatements are good for both background information on a topic and to locate citations to primary materials. Restatements are not law unless they have been adopted in a jurisdiction. They are highly respected by courts and can be used as highly persuasive authority when there is not a primary source on-point. Restatements can be found in both Lexis and Westlaw, and in print.

I. Jury Instructions

Pattern jury instructions provide uniform instructions for juries in criminal and civil matters. Attorneys and judges can use these as a template and modify them to take account the specific facts in a case. These are helpful to researchers because they clearly identify the elements of the claim, criminal charge, or defense. The instructions also provide citations to primary law that underlie the various elements of the legal rule.

The Council of Superior Court Judges of Georgia publishes the *Georgia Suggested Pattern Jury Instructions*. It is comprised of two volumes: the first is on civil matters, and the second is on criminal matters. It is currently in its fifth edition and is updated twice a year. This publication is available digitally at the Georgia Superior Courts website[9], and on Lexis and Westlaw.

The Eleventh Circuit Judicial Council publishes pattern jury instructions for the Eleventh Circuit Court of Appeals. These are available for free at the Eleventh Circuit Court of Appeals' website.[10] Other federal jury instructions are available in *O'Malley, Grenig, & Lee, Federal Jury Practice and*

---

9. *Pattern Jury Instructions*, Georgia Superior Courts, https://georgiasuperior-courts.org/pattern-jury-instructions/ [https://perma.cc/ZY2S-ZFGY].

10. *Pattern Jury Instructions*, United States Court of Appeals for the Eleventh Circuit, www.ca11.uscourts.gov/pattern-jury-instructions [https://perma.cc/V5F6-PUMD].

Instructions published by West and *Modern Federal Jury Instructions* published by Lexis.

III. Using Secondary Sources

Secondary sources are most commonly used in understanding a legal topic or issue. Researchers may consult them to find more resources in a research area. Secondary sources are not typically cited in legal memorandums or filings with a court. However, there are certain times when you may want to cite a secondary source.

It may be useful to cite to a secondary source such as a law review article or a treatise to explain the development of the law on a legal issue or the evolution of the law. There also are situations when there is not a binding law on point or you are attempting to change, expand, or limit the law in your jurisdiction. In these situations, researchers may cite relevant secondary sources to support their position. It is important that researchers critically review the secondary source.

There are several factors to consider when selecting a secondary source to cite in a legal memorandum or court filing. These factors include:

- **Author**: Researchers need to consider who wrote the secondary source. Is the author a prestigious law professor, judge or attorney, or was it authored by a law student or lesser known individual?

- **Type**: Is the citation from a *Restatement of the Law*, a highly respected treatise, from a well-respected law journal, or is it from a continuing legal education (CLE) program or a relatively unknown treatise? The more highly regarded the secondary source the more persuasive it will be.

- **Date of Publication**: In most instances you will want to use secondary sources that are current, so they reflect the current state of the law. There are some circumstances when researchers may want to cite to historical materials, but generally, more recent materials are preferred.

- **Publisher**: Was the secondary source published by a well-established legal publisher such as, the American Bar Association, Wolters Kluwer, Bloomberg Law, Lexis, or West, or is it self-published or from an obscure publisher?

- **Citation**: Has the secondary source been cited previously by courts? If yes, which courts? Researchers should focus on secondary sources that have been cited previously by courts and ideally locate materials cited by appellate courts.

Researchers will need to select among the different types of secondary sources depending on a variety of factors. These include the experience of the researcher in the legal topic, what type of information they are looking for, how much time they have to research, and the availability of the secondary source.

IV. Conclusion

Secondary sources are a key component in the research process, and researchers need to take advantage of them to be efficient in their legal research. There are multiple benefits for starting your research in secondary sources, and these can be accessed online and in print. There are a variety of secondary sources that researchers can use in their research, and they should select the most appropriate secondary source based upon the attributes of each type of secondary source described in this chapter.

Chapter 5

Statutes, Court Rules, and Municipal Ordinances

After reading this chapter you will be able to:

- Describe the differences between session and codified laws;

- Choose effective ways to search Georgia and federal statutes in print and online;

- Select the correct version of a statute; and

- Recognize how to research uniform laws, court rules, and municipal ordinances.

Even though the United States is considered a common law country, statutes play a key role in our legal system because they are the laws made by legislatures. This chapter will focus on researching Georgia and federal statutes and court rules, and will also discuss municipal ordinances in Georgia.

I. Publication of Statutes

A. Georgia Session Laws

Georgia statutes are published in two forms, session laws and codified laws. *Session laws* are all the laws passed by the Georgia General Assembly, referred to as acts or statutes, which are published initially on the state General Assembly website and then are published in print chronologically in an annual publication printed by the State of Georgia entitled *Georgia Laws*. Sometimes research requires reviewing the original text of the act that is printed in this publication. *Georgia Laws* contains acts and resolutions passed since 1787. Some laws, such as local laws, may be published only in *Georgia Laws* and not subsequently codified. Local laws are described more fully below in Section II(B).

Each act passed by the Georgia General Assembly contains a preamble or caption that serves as a *purpose* clause at the beginning of the act. This is commentary that is provided outside of the actual text of the statute, but it assists in determining the intent of the legislature. This purpose clause will not be found in the text of the codified version of the act.

There are several different ways researchers can locate *Georgia Laws*. A print version of the set is available and is organized chronologically by the date the bill was signed by the governor or the date the bill received a two-thirds majority vote in both the State House and Senate following a veto of the bill by the governor. There is also an index that permits researchers to search by the Georgia House or Senate bill number. Table 5-1 provides the location of session laws online.

Table 5-1. Online Coverage of *Georgia Laws*

Database or Website	Coverage
GALILEO – Georgia Legislative Documents[1]	1799–1999
GALILEO – Georgia Government Publications[2]	2000–Present
Georgia Legislature	2000–Present
Fastcase	2010–Present
Lexis	1995–Present
Westlaw	1990–Present

B. Federal Session Laws

Researchers focusing on Georgia law also need to be familiar with federal statutes. Federal laws are published first as slip laws, then as session laws, and

---

1. *Georgia Legislative Documents*, GALILEO www.galileo.usg.edu/express ?link=zlgl [https://perma.cc/JJG2-VQF3].

2. *Georgia Government Publications*, GALILEO, dlg.galileo.usg.edu/cgi/ggpd [https://perma.cc/UD2J-M8AA].

finally as codified laws. The slip laws are individually printed and may be available in federal depository libraries. The session laws are printed in a publication entitled *United States Statutes at Large* (*Statutes at Large*), and like *Georgia Laws*, are organized by the date the president signs the bill or the date the bill received a two-thirds majority vote in both the House and Senate following a veto of the bill by the president. *Statutes at Large* is prepared and published by the Office of the Federal Register, National Archives and Records Administration.

Again, sometimes it is necessary for researchers to review the text of a statute as it appears in the *Statutes at Large*, whether in its original enactment or any applicable amendments to the statute. Please note that the publication of the *Statutes at Large* lags substantially behind acts that have been passed by the federal government. As of the publication of this book, the most recent *Statutes at Large* volume is from 2013. *Statutes at Large* will be available in print at Georgia law libraries, but researchers should contact the law library about its specific holdings. Coverage of the *Statutes at Large* online is set forth in Table 5-2.

Table 5-2. Online Coverage of *Statutes at Large*

Database or Website	Coverage
Govinfo.gov	1951–2013
Lexis	1789–2013
Westlaw	1789–1972

Researchers needing free access to more recent laws will need to go to Congress.gov and review the public laws.[3] Lexis provides the public laws passed by the federal government since 2014. Westlaw has the public laws from 1973 to the present in the *U.S. Code Congressional & Administrative News* (U.S.C.C.A.N.). U.S.C.C.A.N. also contains selected legislative history and administrative materials. Fastcase contains public laws going back to 2015.

---

3. *Public Laws*, Congress.gov, congress.gov/public-laws [https://perma.cc/V6FT -9ZBH].

II. Codification of Statutes

In addition to being printed as session laws, acts of general applicability are published in statutory codes. This codification of statutes permits researchers to locate statutes much more efficiently because they are organized by topics, rather than in chronological order. The codified version of statutes also includes only laws that are currently in effect, which makes it easier for researchers to understand the current law.

Statutory codes can be published with or without annotations. *Annotations* are supplemental information to the text of the statute that are provided by editors. Annotations include citations and summaries of cases interpreting the statutory section, references to secondary materials explaining the statutory section, and cross-references to other statutes and administrative materials that researchers should consult.

A. Official and Unofficial Codes

Statutory codes can be deemed an "official" or an "unofficial" code of a jurisdiction. A code is *official* when a government arranges for the publication of its statutes into a code. This can be published by the government itself or through a commercial vendor such as Lexis or West. Many jurisdictions will also have an unofficial code. This unofficial code is a re-publication of the official code by a third party, usually a commercial publisher. Unofficial codes will contain the exact same text and organization as the official version, and these will be further discussed below.

B. Codification of Georgia Statutes

The session laws of Georgia are codified into an official statutory code published and organized by Lexis in conjunction with the Georgia Code Reviser Office, known as the *Official Code of Georgia Annotated* (O.C.G.A.). The O.C.G.A. currently consists of 53 titles, which are arranged alphabetically except for the first title (General Provisions). The code is organized from the most general to the narrowest, by titles, chapters, articles, parts, subparts, sections, subsections, paragraphs, subparagraphs, divisions, and finally subdivisions, from general to the narrowest.[4] An annotated version of the

---

4. O.C.G.A. § 1-1-8 (2021).

O.C.G.A. is published and freely available at the Georgia Legislature website.[5]

West publishes an annotated code of Georgia entitled, *West's Code of Georgia Annotated*. This unofficial code contains the same text and organization of the statutes as the O.C.G.A., but the West editors select and provide their own annotations. Therefore, researchers will encounter different case summaries and cross-references to other secondary and primary resources within the two versions of the annotated codes.

Codified statutes include only laws of general applicability. Local and special acts are not included in the code and are published only in volume II of *Georgia Laws* for the year in which they were passed. A *local act* is a measure that applies to a specific city, county, or special district named in the act. However, *Georgia Laws* includes an index of the local laws for each legislative session. The O.C.G.A. includes a cumulative index for these local and special acts in volumes 42 and 42A of the print edition of the O.C.G.A.

i. Official Code of Georgia Annotated

During a special session in 1981, the Georgia General Assembly adopted the *Official Code of Georgia Annotated* (O.C.G.A.), which was a joint effort by Michie Company (later purchased by Lexis) and the Georgia General Assembly. The O.C.G.A. became effective on November 1, 1982.[6] "A three-unit numbering system is used to designate [code] sections."[7] For example, O.C.G.A. Section 3-2-5 refers to Section 5, in Chapter 2, of Title 3 of the

---

5. *LexisNexis Custom Solution*, Georgia General Assembly, www.lexisnexis.com/hottopics/gacode [https://perma.cc/YCG7-YVZQ].

6. For a summary of the history on the development of the codification of the Georgia statutes see, State of Georgia, *History of the Codification of the Laws of Georgia O.C.G.A.* xiii–xv (2007); Terry A. McKennie, *The Making of a New Code*, 18 Ga. St. B.J. 102 (1982). Prior to the codification of Georgia statutes, they were organized into digests and compilations. These were published between 1799–1859. These early publications are available through Digital Commons, the institutional repository of the University of Georgia School of Law which is provided by the Alexander Campbell King Law Library, digitalcommons.law.uga.edu/ga_code/ [https://perma.cc/YEA6-2L9T.]

7. *User's guide to the Official Code of Georgia Annotated*, www.legis.ga.gov/api/document/docs/default-source/lc-resources/user's-guide-to-the-official-code-of-georgia-annotated1.pdf?sfvrsn=bd4e3b0f_2 [https://perma.cc/5C9A-32N2].

O.C.G.A. Researchers will see gaps between some parts, articles, chapters or sections to account for future legislation.[8]

The second most recent code version is the 1933 *Code of Georgia*, which was amended up through the creation of the 1981 Code. You will recognize a citation to the 1933 Code because citations are formatted as two numbers separated by a hyphen, such as XX-XXX. The number before the hyphen, XX in this example, refers to the chapter. The number after the hyphen, XXX in this example, refers to the section. Other prior codes include the 1926 Code, 1910 Code, 1895 Code, and further codes or compilations of laws that date back to 1799. Many of these historical versions of the code are available freely online through the Alexander Campbell King Law Library at the University of Georgia School of Law.[9]

Occasionally researchers will need to locate statutes from previous versions of the Georgia code. The print version of the O.C.G.A. contains tables that convert citations to code sections from prior code versions to the 1981 code (as amended) as well as from the 1981 code to prior code versions. This is located in Volume 41 of the O.C.G.A.

ii. *Code of Georgia Annotated*

Originally published by Harrison Company, the *Code of Georgia Annotated* is an unofficial Georgia Code published in 1933 and continuing as *West's Code of Georgia Annotated*, after West purchased Harrison in 2003. The *West's Code of Georgia Annotated* contains the same statutory language as the O.C.G.A., but the editorial enhancements vary. These enhancements include annotations such as cases, related references, cross references, and citations to secondary sources that may be relevant to a given code section. Note that *West's Code of Georgia Annotated* does not include the index to local and special acts or the table to convert current code sections to previous versions of the Georgia code.

C. Codification of Federal Statutes

The federal session laws are organized by topic into the *United States Code* by the Office of the Law Revision Counsel of the United States House of Representatives. These are currently organized into 54 titles by topic however,

---

8. *Id.*

9. *Historic Digests and Codes*, Digital Commons, digitalcommons.law.uga.edu/ ga_code [https://perma.cc/4B2A-35KM].

additional titles may be added in the future. The federal code can be found in three different publications, one official unannotated code and two unofficial annotated codes, which are discussed below.

i. United States Code (U.S.C.)

The U.S.C. is the official code published by the Government Publishing Office. This code contains no annotations. The U.S.C. was originally published in 1926 and a new edition of the code has been issued every six years since 1934, with the most recent issuance occurring in 2018. Annual supplements are published to bring the U.S.C. up to date between publication of each edition. Like session laws, these supplements substantially lag behind current legislation, so researchers will miss current laws and amendments if they solely rely on the U.S.C. The U.S.C. is also available at the govinfo website.[10] The print and online versions of the U.S.C. do not contain recent laws and amendments, and researchers will need to consult Congress.gov or unofficial sources for more current information.

The U.S.C. includes the text of statutes and historical information about the statutory sections. The U.S.C. uses a two-unit numbering system to designate code sections consisting of the title and section. For example, the citation 5 U.S.C. § 528, refers to title 5, section 528 in the United States Code.

ii. The United States Code Service, Lawyers Edition (U.S.C.S.)

The U.S.C.S. is an unofficial code published by Lexis. This publication includes the 54 titles of the U.S.C., the United States Constitution, Federal Court Rules, and selected supplemental primary sources. The statutes include historical information about their enactment and any amendments. Lexis editors provide annotations to the statutes which include judicial and administrative decisions interpreting the statute and cross references to applicable primary and secondary materials.

iii. The United States Code Annotated (U.S.C.A.)

The U.S.C.A. is an unofficial code published by West. This is also an annotated code that includes the 54 Titles of the U.S.C., the United States Constitution, and Federal Court Rules. The statutes will include historical information about their enactment and any amendments. West editors

---

10. *United States Code*, govinfo, govinfo.gov/app/collection/uscode [https:// perma.cc/7GYK-DPHJ].

provide annotations of cases that include judicial (but not administrative) decisions interpreting the statute, cross references to applicable primary and secondary materials, and historical information regarding the amendment of the statute over time.

III. Citation of Statutes

Citation of statutes is discussed in rule 12 of *The Bluebook* and rule 14 of the *Guide to Legal Citation by Association of Legal Writing Directors* (ALWD). Section 1-1-8(e) of the Official Code of Georgia Annotated permits citation to the Official Code of Georgia Annotated as "O.C.G.A." rather than as "Ga. Code Ann.," which is used by *The Bluebook* and *ALWD*. Thus, a citation to Georgia statutes in Georgia legal materials almost always appears as O.C.G.A. § 1-1-8, and researchers may see the same statute cited as Ga. Code. Ann. § 1-1-8 in legal materials from other jurisdictions.

Federal statutes are cited according to the reporters listed in Table 1 of *The Bluebook* in accordance with rule 12 of *The Bluebook* and rule 14 of *ALWD*.

IV. Researching Print Codes

A. Locating Statutes

Whether you are using the print version of the O.C.G.A or *West's Code of Georgia Annotated*, U.S.C., U.S.C.S., or U.S.C.A., the search process will be the same. However, please note that the U.S.C. will not be as up to date as the unofficial versions of the federal code.

There are four different methods to locate relevant statutes in print. Remember, researchers should first start with secondary sources if they are not familiar with the legal topic or issue. If you have a citation to a statute from a secondary source or otherwise, you can simply locate the relevant statutory section using the citation.

If researchers know the name of a statute, such as the Dairy Act, they can use the Short Title Index (O.C.G.A.) or the Popular Names Table (*West's Code of Georgia Annotated* and U.S.C.A.) or the Popular Names Table (U.S.C.S.) to locate a citation to the statute based on its name. The Table will include a list of all the sections of a law, as laws may be codified in various titles.

The next method involves consulting a code's table of contents to locate relevant statutes. Researchers can browse the code's table of contents to identify the correct statutory topic in an applicable title, and then further browse the table of contents set forth in the title to locate relevant chapters and other subdivisions within the title. Researchers will most likely need to have some experience in the legal topic to be effective in this method.

The last way to locate relevant statutes in print is by using an index. Both Lexis and West publish an index to their print versions of the Georgia and federal codes, and these are updated on an annual basis. Researchers can use the terms they developed in the research plan discussed in Chapter 2 to locate applicable entries in the indexes. These indexes will then provide citations to the appropriate statutes.

B. Updating Print Statutes

Researchers need to confirm that they are using the correct version of the statute. Much of the time researchers are looking for the version of the law that is currently in effect, but sometimes a researcher needs an earlier version of the law. Instructions on researching previous versions of a statute are below in the section Versions of a Statute.

Both Lexis and West update the print versions of their statutory Georgia and federal codes through pocket parts and soft bound supplements. Pocket parts are inserted at the end of hard bound volumes and will contain updates for any new legislation or amendments to a statutory section and provide new annotations. There are also soft bound supplements that will be found at the end of the statutory code containing new legislation and annotations. A soft-bound supplement is used when the pocket part no longer fits in the back of the main volume. When reading a statute, researchers will need to determine if there are any pocket parts or soft bound supplements that contain changes to the statute. If there are no changes shown in the pocket part, the language of the main volume is current. The U.S.C. also provides annual supplements, but as of the publication of this book, the most recent print supplement was issued in 2018.

V. Versions of a Statute

If the legal issue arises from an action that occurred prior to the current version of the statute, the researcher will need to determine and locate the version of the statute was in effect when the issue arose. Researchers can use the history section of a statute to see when a statute was enacted and view citation information for any subsequent amendments. If an amendment to the statute occurred after the incident, researchers will need to review the historical version of the statute to see what language existed during the relevant time period. Annotated codes, such as the O.C.G.A., West's Code of Georgia Annotated, the U.S.C.S., and the U.S.C.A., contain expanded information describing the historical revisions to statutes, which are quite helpful in making this evaluation efficiently. An example of the history section of a Georgia statute is shown in Figure 5.1.

Figure 5.1. History Section of Georgia Statute[11]

History
Ga. L. 1937, p. 746, § 3; Ga. L. 1982, p. 3, § 44; Ga. L. 2016, p. 193, § 7/HB 1004.

This information displays that this statutory section was originally enacted in 1937 and the act can be found on page 746, section 3, of the 1937 *Georgia Laws*. This also provides that the statutory section was amended in 1982, and this act is printed in the 1982 *Georgia Laws* on page 3, section 44. The most recent amendment to this statutory section occurred in 2016 and can be found in the 2016 *Georgia Laws* on page 193, section 7. If the events giving rise to the legal issue happened in 2014, the version of the law that would be controlling would be the one published in the 1982 *Georgia Laws*. On the other hand, if the events giving rise to the legal issue happened in 2017, the current version of the law would be controlling. Table 5-1 contains a list of websites and databases for consulting *Georgia Laws*.

---

11. Source: O.C.G.A. § 44-2-28 (2021), www.lexisnexis.com/hottopics/gacode [https://perma.cc/YCG7-YVZQ].

Just like O.C.G.A. and *West's Code of Georgia Annotated*, the U.S.C., U.S.C.A. and U.S.C.S. will contain a history section on the statute that will provide when it was enacted and amended. An example of a history section of a federal statute is displayed below:

(Pub. L. 87–443, §2, Apr. 27, 1962, 76 Stat. 62; Pub. L. 94–209, Feb. 5, 1976, 90 Stat. 30.)

The historical information will be the same in all versions of the federal code. Researchers can see that this statutory section was enacted on April 27, 1962, and the text can be found in volume 76 of *Statutes at Large* on page 62. This statute was amended on February 5, 1976, and the text can be found in volume 90 of *Statutes at Large* on page 30. Researchers can consult the applicable *Statutes at Large* pages through the various websites and databases listed in Table 5-2.

Sometimes it is necessary to review the codified version of a statute, chapter or article rather than only the text of a specific amendment or enactment. Those researchers need to consult the previous versions of the entire statutory code. Historical versions of the O.C.G.A., *West's Code of Georgia Annotated*, U.S.C., U.S.C.A. and U.S.C.S. are most often consulted in electronic form when possible. Law libraries may have print or microform versions of historical codes, but researchers will need to check the specific dates available for the codes being researched. Online versions of current and historical Georgia codes are available as set forth in Table 5-3, and Table 5-4 displays the coverage of online versions of current and historical historic federal codes.

Table 5-3. Online Access to Georgia Codes

Database or Website	Coverage of Historical Georgia Codes
Fastcase (O.C.G.A. – text only)	2009–Present
Lexis (O.C.G.A.)	1991–Present
Westlaw (West's *Code of Georgia Annotated*)	2002–Present
University of Georgia School of Law Digital Commons (Historic Georgia Codes)	1860–1933

Table 5-4. Online Access to Federal Codes

Database or Website	Coverage
Govinfo.gov (U.S.C.)	1994–2018
Fastcase (U.S.C.)	2006, 2010–Present
Lexis (U.S.C.S.)	1992–Present
Westlaw (U.S.C.A.)	1990–Present

VI. Validating Statutes

When researching statutes, researchers also need to ensure the statute is still good law. Researchers must verify that the statute has not been deemed unconstitutional, voided or invalidated by a judicial opinion, superseded by new legislation, and review pending legislation affecting the statute.

If using print statutes, researchers will need to consult the citator provided by either Lexis or Westlaw to confirm the validity of a statute. Although Lexis publishes a print version of Shepard's Georgia Citations and Shepard's Federal Statute Citations, very few law firms or law libraries subscribe to these publications, and they are not as current as online options.

Lexis and Westlaw each have their own online citator services to determine if a statute is still good law. Lexis offers Shepard's to check the status of primary materials, while Westlaw offers KeyCite for this purpose. The use of these citators is discussed more fully in Chapter 11.

VII. Researching Codes Online

There are advantages to researching codes online versus print. Sources for the various Georgia and federal codes are displayed in Table 5-3 and Table 5-4. Researchers can use the same methods to locate applicable statutes discussed previously: by citation, by popular name, browsing the table of contents, and using the index, though the availability of the options varies by source. West makes its index and popular names tables available online for all of its statutory codes in Westlaw. Lexis makes its popular name table available for the federal code online, and it provides an online index to the O.C.G.A. However, there is not an index or popular name table available in other codes provided online, whether by the Georgia General Assembly, govinfo.gov, or Fastcase. Researchers do have the benefit of using natural language, keyword, or terms and connector searching to locate relevant statutes within all of these websites and databases. Check the website instructions for information on how to effectively search the site, as connectors and search functionality varies.

When conducting searches for statutes, researchers need their searches to be general and anticipate the language that the Georgia General Assembly or Congress used in drafting the statute. Note that when searching in Lexis and Westlaw, a search in a statutes database source will default to search for terms within annotations to the statutes as well as the language of the statute itself. Researchers can use advanced search tools available on the commercial database platforms, including Lexis, Westlaw, and Fastcase, to make their searches more effective. The advanced search tools vary by provider and providers include instructions to assist users in searching efficiently within each database.

A. Selecting the Version, Updating, and Validating Online Statutes

Just like print versions of the code, researchers need to determine that they are using the correct version of the statutory section. The online Georgia and federal codes, whether on the Georgia General Assembly website, Fastcase, Lexis, or Westlaw, are continuously updated, so researchers do not need to consult pocket parts or softbound statutory supplements. Premium databases such as Lexis, Westlaw, and Fastcase include information about the currentness of the information available.

Laws in Georgia, unless otherwise designated by the legislature, go into effect on July 1 of the year in which they were passed. Barring a special legislative session, Georgia statutes cannot be amended after the last day of the legislative session. For example, if the legislative session ends on April 15, and there is no special legislative session, there can be no amendment to the code until the commencement of the next legislative session. In that example, the 'current-through' date for the Georgia statutes would be listed as April 15 for the rest of the calendar year. To check whether a statute has been amended since the 'current-through' date, the researcher consults the legislature's website to see whether any new legislation amending that statute has been passed. If the citator (consulted when validating the statute) did not indicate any pending legislation, it is unlikely that a statute would have been amended.

If the legal issue arises from a past incident, researchers will need to use the historical version of the code, if the past version of the statute varies from the current version. The same historical information about a statute section's enactment and any amendments are also included in the online version. Premium databases provided by Lexis and Westlaw offer hyperlinks to the pages in *Georgia Laws* and *Statutes at Large*. Additional electronic versions of the Georgia historical codes are set forth in Table 5-3, and federal historical codes are set forth in Table 5-4.

Both Lexis and Westlaw have features that allow researchers to see how a statutory section has changed between two different years. Once a researcher finds an applicable statute, the researcher can click on "Compare Versions" link and select the years she would like to compare and both services will provide a comparison of the terms and provisions that were added or removed from the statutory section.

Just as when using print to locate statutes, researchers will need to consult a citator and review any Shepard's or KeyCite signals, as discussed above in Validating Statutes.

VIII. Statutory Annotations

Both print and online versions of the Georgia and federal statutes contain additional references to primary materials and secondary sources, which are called annotations. The same annotations selected by Lexis and West editors for the print versions of their respective codes are available in the online versions.

In Lexis, annotations of cases that have cited to the statute follow the text of a statute labelled "Case Notes" or "Notes to Decisions." Westlaw includes the case annotations for statutes on the "Notes of Decision" tab. In print, annotations of cases relevant to the statute are labelled "Notes of Decisions." Researchers can find additional cases, and other primary and secondary materials that have cited to a statute by checking the citator analysis of the statute. This is discussed in detail in Chapter 11.

Annotations also include other sources that the editorial staff of the publisher have identified as potentially helpful to the researcher. However, Lexis and Westlaw will recommend only sources that they make available in their respective databases. These recommended sources may include additional statutes, related regulations, and law review articles or other secondary sources.

Another type of annotation to a statute consists of notes regarding the history of changes to the statute. Although the official version of a statute includes the brief history of the amendments to the law over time (as discussed in Section V above), unofficial publishers include more detailed descriptions of the specific changes. These more detailed notes can save a researcher time consulting prior versions, as it is easier to identify whether amendments were not relevant to the legal issue being researched.

IX. Reading Statutes

Even when researchers find an appropriate statutory section and determines it is good law, they must take further steps. The most critical step is to read the statute carefully, taking into account all of the subparts of a statutory section. The O.C.G.A. has a statute on the construction of statutes generally in O.C.G.A. § 1-3-1:

(a) In all interpretations of statutes, the courts shall look diligently for the intention of the General Assembly, keeping in view at all times the old law, the evil, and the remedy. Grammatical errors shall not vitiate a law. A transposition of words and clauses may be resorted to when a sentence or clause is without meaning as it stands.

(b) In all interpretations of statutes, the ordinary signification shall be applied to all words, except words of art or words connected with a particular trade or subject matter, which shall have the signification attached to them by experts in such trade or with reference to such subject matter.

(c) A substantial compliance with any statutory requirement, especially on the part of public officers, shall be deemed and held sufficient, and no proceeding shall be declared void for want of such compliance, unless expressly so provided by law.

There are other subparts in O.C.G.A. § 1-3-1 that address statutes on bonds, census, computation of time, and specific terms. The federal code also addresses rules of construction in 1 U.S.C. §§ 1-8, but these sections focus on specific terms used in the U.S.C. For example, the singular form includes the plural, "county" includes a parish, "company" includes its successors and assigns, etc.

Researchers also need to review the table of contents to ensure that they are not missing any statutory sections that affect their legal issue. These other statutory sections may contain definitions of terms, exceptions, penalties, procedural matters, and other information that will be critical in resolving the legal issue and understating the statute. These relevant sections are often found in the same 'neighborhood', or portion of the code, as laws on the same topic are codified near to each other.

Many times, researchers will not be able to interpret or understand the statute controlling their legal issue based solely on the text of the statute and its surrounding sections. Researchers will need to also consult the annotations, and other primary materials citing to the statute, to help them interpret and understand the statute.

Lastly, researchers can consult the various "canons of construction" that have been established by Georgia and federal courts to assist in interpreting statutes.[12] These canons will assist researchers in interpreting the text, grammar, syntax, and presumptions of statutes with rules established by courts. Examples include "Expressio unius est exclusio alterius" or the express mention of one thing implies the exclusion of another, "ejusdem generis" or general statements only apply to the same kind of persons or things specifically listed, and to avoid interpretations that would render a statute unconstitutional, among other rules.

X. Uniform Laws

There are a number of Georgia statutes that are based upon uniform laws drafted by the Uniform Law Commission ("ULC"). The ULC was established in 1892 and its purpose is to "draft uniform state laws in areas of state law where uniformity is desirable and practical."[13] ULC members must be qualified to practice law and are comprised of lawyers, judges, law professors,

---

12. Norman J. Singer, *Sutherland's Status and Statutory Construction* (8th ed. 2018) (federal and state statute canons); William N. Eskridge, Jr. & Philip P. Frickey, *Foreword: Law as Equilibrium*, 108 Harv. L. Rev. 26, 97–108 (2014) (federal statutes); R. Perry Sentell, *The Canons of Construction in Georgia: "Anachronisms" in Action*, 25 Ga. L. Rev. 365 (1991).

13. Uniform Law Commission, *Overview*, Uniform Law Commission: Better Laws. Stronger States, https://www.uniformlaws.org/aboutulc/overview [https://perma.cc/H29W-995S].

legislators, and others. These individuals are appointed by state governments, the District of Columbia, Puerto Rico, and the U.S. Virgin Islands.[14] There are over 150 uniform acts that have been drafted by the ULC, but the number of states passing an act various substantially. Some of the more well-known and widely implemented acts include the Uniform Commercial Code (UCC), the Uniform Probate Act, and the Uniform Trade Secrets Act.

These uniform statutes are compiled and annotated in a publication entitled *Uniform Laws Annotated*, published by West. This publication provides the text of all of the uniform laws together with annotations to assist researchers in interpreting and understanding the applicable uniform law. This publication also provides information about the states that have enacted the uniform law, text variances in a state's adoption of the statute, notes from the drafters on the act, summaries of cases interpreting the statute, and cross-references to relevant primary and secondary materials.

This publication is available in print and on Westlaw. The online and the print versions of the title do not perfectly mirror each other. The version in Westlaw uses KeyCite to provide annotations to primary and secondary materials that cite to the Uniform Law. The print version of a state code that has adopted a Uniform Law includes details about other jurisdictions that have adopted the law. Westlaw provides variations in the text between the uniform law and the version enacted by a state, while the online version does not. Lexis has the text and comments from the drafters of the uniform acts, but it does not have the annotations and it does not permit Shepardizing of the uniform law.

When reviewing a Georgia statute, researchers may find that the statute is based on a uniform law. If the researcher has difficulty in finding Georgia primary materials that interpret the statute based on the legal issue, then the researcher can look to other jurisdictions that have also passed the uniform law with the same language as persuasive authority. Researchers can determine the other relevant jurisdictions by reviewing the *Uniform Laws Annotated* or by consulting the Uniform Law Commission website[15] and locating citations to the statutes passed by other states. Once researchers have the citation, they can locate these statutes using Fastcase, Lexis, or Westlaw.

---

14. *Id.*

15. Uniform Law Commission, *Uniform Law Commission: Better Laws. Stronger States*, https://www.uniformlaws.org/home [https://perma.cc/S68B-QWGD].

XI. Court Rules

Court rules are the rules that generally govern the procedures followed by a particular court, specifically the procedures about how the court manages its business. The Georgia legislature, over time, has passed into law a number of provisions governing the rules of evidence as well as civil and criminal practice. These provisions are codified in Title 24, Title 9, and Title 17 of the O.C.G.A. respectively. Some of these laws are analogous to the Federal Rules of Evidence, Rules of Civil Procedure, and Rules of Criminal Procedure.

In addition to the rules which may be found in the O.C.G.A., Georgia courts promulgate their own rules. These rules address requirements that are specific to particular courts in particular jurisdictions and may include, for example, content-based filing requirements[16] or set forth requirements for filings in particular types of actions such as domestic relations matters.[17] However, the rules promulgated by the courts are not meant to conflict with substantive law (that is made by the legislature) or the Georgia Constitution.[18]

In Georgia, most levels of courts have their own rules including uniform rules for courts such as the superior courts, state courts, juvenile courts, probate courts, magistrate courts, and municipal courts. For the lower courts, the rules are uniform, which standardizes the process of appearing before courts throughout Georgia, although courts' internal operating procedures relating to things such as case assignment, court administration, or grand jury management, that are not susceptible to uniformity, may still vary by court.[19] Rules for the Georgia Supreme Court, Court of Appeals, and the State-Wide Business Court are unique to each court and are not described as uniform, since there is only one of each of those courts.

West's Code of Georgia Annotated includes court rules and related annotations. The O.C.G.A. does not include Georgia court rules; they are instead available in print from Lexis in a separate volume called *Georgia Rules of Court Annotated*. The *Georgia Rules of Court* is also annotated. Premium databases include the Georgia rules of court and related annotations. Free

---

16. Ga. Unif. Super. Ct. R. 6.1.
17. Ga. Unif. Super. Ct. R. 24.
18. Ga. Unif. Super. Ct. R. 1.
19. Ga. Unif. Super. Ct. R. 1.2.

sources for the rules of court include the Administrative Office of the Courts and individual courts themselves, such as the Supreme Court of Georgia.

Federal courts follow their own rules. These include rules on civil and criminal procedure, evidence, appellate, bankruptcy and other rules. *Georgia Court Rules and Procedure—Federal* includes federal court rules in print, as do the U.S.C., U.S.C.A., and U.S.C.S. The federal court rules included in the annotated codes (U.S.C.A. and U.S.C.S.) are annotated with cases that have interpreted the rules and other information that researchers find helpful. Federal appellate and district courts also may have *local rules* that attorneys must follow. The local rules applicable in federal courts are similar in content to the uniform rules in Georgia trial courts. Federal appellate courts also have local rules that guide the business of the courts. These local court rules are freely available on court websites. See Table 5-5 for a listing of federal courts and links to their local rules.

Table 5-5. Federal Courts and Website Addresses for Local Court Rules

Name of Court	Website Address for Court Rules
United States District Court, Northern District of Georgia	gand.uscourts.gov/local-rules
United States Bankruptcy Court, Northern District of Georgia	ganb.uscourts.gov/local-rules-and-orders
United States District Court, Middle District of Georgia	gamd.uscourts.gov/local-rules
United States Bankruptcy Court, Middle District of Georgia	gamb.uscourts.gov/USCourts/local-rules-and-clerks-instructions
United States District Court, Southern District of Georgia	gasd.uscourts.gov/court-info/local-rules-and-orders
United States Bankruptcy Court, Southern District of Georgia	gasb.uscourts.gov/local-rules
Court of Appeals, 11th Circuit	ca11.uscourts.gov/rules-procedures
United States Supreme Court	supremecourt.gov/filingandrules/rules_guidance.aspx

XII. Municipal Ordinances

Under the "Home Rule," the Georgia Constitution grants cities and counties the ability to adopt "reasonable ordinances, resolutions, or regulations relating to its property, affairs, and local government for which no provision has been made by general law and which is not inconsistent with this Constitution or any local law."[20] Municipal ordinances focus on a variety of topics including public health and safety, licenses, fees, criminal offenses, taxes, zoning, and building codes.

Researchers should first consult Municode, municode.com, a free resource, to locate Georgia county and city ordinances. These ordinances can be viewed by browsing the table of contents or through keyword searching. Researchers should note when the ordinances have last been updated within Municode because there may have been additional ordinances adopted since it was last updated at this website. If the applicable county or city does not have its ordinances on Municode, or if updated ordinances are needed, then researchers should review the county or city website.

XIII. Conclusion

Statutes are first published chronologically as session laws and then organized into codes so that researchers can more effectively locate applicable statutes. Researchers may use different methods to locate statutes based upon their legal research project and their knowledge of the legal topic. After locating an applicable statute, researchers need to determine that they are using the applicable version and use a citator to update the statute and ensure that it is good law. Lastly, uniform laws, court rules, and municipal ordinances may need to be reviewed when researching a legal issue.

---

20. Ga Const. art. IX § 2.

Chapter 6

Judicial Opinions

After this chapter you will be able to:

- Select a binding case;
- Distinguish between "published" and "unpublished" cases;
- Identify the parts of a case; and
- Recognize different ways to locate cases.

Researching judicial opinions is important in legal research. These decisions issued by courts interpret statutes and administrative materials and also apply and develop a jurisdiction's common law. This chapter will discuss the selection of judicial opinions, the publication of judicial opinions, the different parts of a judicial opinion, the citation of judicial opinions, and different ways to locate them.

I. Selecting Binding Cases

When researchers are conducting case law research they need to ensure that they are selecting cases that are binding. Generally, in order for a judicial opinion to be binding, it must be from the controlling jurisdiction and from a higher court. As discussed in Chapter 1, there are three levels of courts in the Georgia court system, trial courts, which consists of general and limited jurisdiction courts; the Court of Appeals of Georgia; and the Georgia Supreme Court. The federal court system also consists of three levels, the federal trial courts (including United States District Courts, United States Bankruptcy Courts, United States Court of International Claims, and United States Tax Courts), the United States Courts of Appeals, and the United States Supreme Court.

If an issue involves Georgia state law, then researchers need to review cases from a higher Georgia state court, which could be a Court of Appeals of Georgia decision or a Georgia Supreme Court decision. Georgia Supreme Court decisions will be binding law to the Court of Appeals of Georgia and Georgia trial courts, and Court of Appeals of Georgia decisions will also be binding on Georgia trial courts. The Georgia Court of Appeals may overrule its previous decisions if certain requirements are met.[1]

Judicial opinions from other jurisdictions, whether from state or federal court, even if involving Georgia law, will not be binding on Georgia courts. The exception to this rule is a federal court holding that Georgia law is unconstitutional under the United States Constitution. Judicial opinions from other jurisdictions involving Georgia law are only persuasive authority on Georgia courts, Georgia courts have the ultimate authority to determine Georgia law as long as it complies with United States Constitution.

If practicing in Georgia and researching a federal law issue, researchers need to review cases that are binding on Georgia federal district courts. This includes decisions from the Eleventh Circuit Court of Appeals and the United States Supreme Court. There is one major caveat. Georgia used to be in the Fifth Circuit Court of Appeals. In 1981, Congress established the Eleventh Circuit Court of Appeals to hear federal cases originating in Alabama, Florida, and Georgia. The Eleventh Circuit Court of Appeals held that "decisions of the United States Court of Appeals for the Fifth Circuit, as that court existed on September 30, 1981, handed down by that court prior to the close of business on that date, shall be binding as precedent in the Eleventh Circuit, for this court, the district courts, and the bankruptcy courts in the circuit."[2] Therefore, decisions from the Fifth Circuit Court of Appeals issued before October 1, 1981 will be binding on the Eleventh Circuit Court of Appeals and Georgia federal district courts. Decisions from other Circuit Courts of Appeals are only persuasive authority for Georgia federal district courts. Only decisions from the Eleventh Circuit, Fifth Circuit decisions issued prior

---

1. "Prior decisions of the Court may be overruled by a single division of the Court after consultation with the other nondisqualified judges on the Court, provided the decision of the division is unanimous. Otherwise, prior decisions of the Court may be overruled after en banc consideration of all nondisqualified judges of the Court by a majority of the participating judges. *See* O.C.G.A. § 15-3-1(d) (2021) (authorizing the Court of Appeals to provide by rule the manner in which prior decisions of the Court may be overruled)." Ga. Ct. App. R. 33.3.

2. *Bonner v. City of Prichard*, 661 F.2d 1206, 1209 (11th Cir. 1981) (en banc).

to October 1, 1981, and United States Supreme Court decisions will binding authority.

Even if the decision is from the correct jurisdiction, researchers also need to consider whether the decision has been "published" by the court.

II. Publication of Judicial Opinions

Researchers need to understand the difference between published decisions (sometimes referred to as reported decisions) and unpublished decisions (sometimes referred to as unreported decisions). Unpublished opinions are now routinely available in online sources, which is potentially confusing to researchers. All of the United States Supreme Court opinions are published, as are most state supreme court decisions, although there are some state supreme court decisions designated as unpublished.

Judges have the discretion to designate their decisions to be published (for publication) or unpublished (not for publication). There are a variety of reasons that judges elect to publish a decision, including whether the decision (i) establishes a new rule of law; (ii) applies a rule of law to a new set of facts; (iii) creates or resolves a conflict of authority, or (iv) explains, criticizes, or reviews the history of existing law.[3] However, the criteria for how a court decides whether to designate an opinion to be published will vary from jurisdiction to jurisdiction. Most of the cases heard by courts are not changing, creating, or developing the law, and this results in courts designating only a small percentage of decisions to be published.

A. Publication Practices by Jurisdiction

Federal and state appellate courts decide whether to publish their opinions based on rules established by each circuit or jurisdiction. These courts also have their own rules on the weight of authority for unpublished opinions. The rules regarding published/unpublished opinions, and the weight of authority for unpublished opinions for the jurisdictions directly effecting Georgia legal research are set forth below. Researchers will need to review

---

3. *See* 5th Cir. R. 47.5.1. In the 11th Circuit Court of Appeals, the majority of the panel of judges hearing a matter make the determination whether the opinion should have precedential value and therefore should be published. 11th Cir. R. 36-2 and I.O.P. 7 (following the rule).

the applicable statutes or rules when researching the case law of other jurisdictions.

1. Georgia Courts

The Supreme Court of Georgia and the Court of Appeals of Georgia each elect whether their decisions will be published or unpublished. Any unpublished decision will not be binding precedent.[4]

2. Federal/Eleventh Circuit

An Eleventh Circuit Court of Appeals decision will be "unpublished unless a majority of the panel decides to publish it. Unpublished opinions are not considered binding precedent, but they may be cited as persuasive authority."[5] The Eleventh Circuit Court of Appeals generally disfavors publishing opinions.[6] Federal district courts in Georgia have the ability to designate a decision for publication, and West may publish these decisions in the *Federal Supplement*.

B. Unpublished Opinions

Researchers will realize that "unpublished" decisions are a bit of a misnomer because these decisions will be found in the *Federal Appendix*[7] and in online legal databases like Lexis and Westlaw. When researchers are using online services, researchers will certainly find judicial opinions that have been deemed "Not for Publication." Again, researchers need to review the rules of precedent with respect to these unpublished opinions within the relevant jurisdiction. Cases may be designated as unpublished, but local court

---

4. Ga. Ct. App. R. 33(b); O.C.G.A. § 5-6-7 (2021).

5. 11th Cir. R. 36-2.

6. 11th Cir I.O.P.36-2(5) "The policy of the court is: The unlimited proliferation of published opinions is undesirable because it tends to impair the development of the cohesive body of law. To meet this serious problem it is declared to be the basic policy of this court to exercise imaginative and innovative resourcefulness in fashioning new methods to increase judicial efficiency and reduce the volume of published opinions. Judges of this court will exercise appropriate discipline to reduce the length of opinions by the use of those techniques which result in brevity without sacrifice of quality."

7. In 2001, West began the publication of the *Federal Appendix*, a case reporter that published "unpublished" federal decisions. Joseph L. Gerken, *A Librarian's Guide to Unpublished Judicial Opinions*, 96 Law Libr. J. 475 (2004). West stopped publishing the *Federal Appendix* in 2021.

rules may allow the unpublished opinions to be cited as persuasive authority.

Researchers using Lexis or Westlaw will have the option to filter their case search results by "reported" or "unreported." Unreported cases are those designated as unpublished by the issuing court. When using Lexis or Westlaw, researchers will know that a case is unpublished because it will cite to the *Federal Appendix*, or it will not have a citation to a reporter listed in Table 1.3 of *The Bluebook*. Citations to unpublished decisions in Lexis or Westlaw may look similar to 2009 U.S. Dist. LEXIS 17073 or 2011 WL 5870059.

C. Publication of Judicial Opinions

Judicial opinions that are selected by a court to be published are printed chronologically in publications generally referred to as *reporters*. Reporters can be organized by jurisdiction, such as the *Georgia Reporter*; topically, such as the *Education Law Reporter*; or by region, such as the *South Eastern Reporter*. Additionally, reporters can be referred to as "official" or "unofficial."

Official reporters are those deemed by a jurisdiction through a statute or other rule to be the official reporter for that jurisdiction. Unofficial reporters are printed by commercial publishers and will have the same cases with the exact same text, but also include publisher provided editorial enhancements to the cases, including synopses, topics and key numbers, and headnotes, all of which assist researchers. Official reporters normally do not contain these editorial enhancements.[8] These editorial enhancements will be discussed later in this chapter in II(f).

D. Georgia Judicial Opinions

Georgia appellate and supreme court decisions designated for publication are published in two different official publications issued by the State of Georgia. Georgia Court of Appeals's decisions are published chronologically in *Georgia Appeals Reports*, and the Supreme Court of Georgia's decisions are published chronologically in *Georgia Reports*.

West also publishes the unofficial *South Eastern Reporter* (1887–current) and *Georgia Cases* (1950–current). These reporters contain decisions by the Supreme Court of Georgia and the Court of Appeals of Georgia. In addition

---

8. *California Official Reports* published by Lexis is an example of an official reporter that includes editorial enhancements.

to Georgia courts, the *South Eastern Reporter* contains the decisions of the appellate and supreme courts of South Carolina, North Carolina, Virginia and West Virginia. *Georgia Cases* contains only the Georgia cases that were published in the *South Eastern Reporter*, including identical editorial enhancements to assist researchers.

Reporters are published in multivolume sets, numbered consecutively. When a set is complete, which may occur when there are 99 volumes, for others when there are 999 volumes, a new series of the same title begins. The *South Eastern Reporter* is currently in the second series and is abbreviated S.E.2d in citations. When the set of the second series is complete after volume 999, the citation will be S.E.3d, for the third series.

Researchers should note that West publishes seven unofficial regional reporters for state appellate and supreme court decisions that contain editorial enhancements. These are set forth in the Table 6-1.

Table 6-1. West Regional Reporter System

Reporter	Reporter Abbreviation	States
Atlantic Reporter	A.	Connecticut, Delaware, Maine, Maryland, New Hampshire, New Jersey, Pennsylvania, Rhode Island, Vermont, & the D.C. Municipal Court of Appeals
	A.2d	
	A.3d	
North Eastern Reporter	N.E.	Illinois, Indiana, Massachusetts, New York & Ohio
	N.E.2d	
North Western Reporter	N.W.	Iowa, Michigan, Minnesota, Nebraska, North Dakota, South Dakota & Wisconsin
	N.W.2d	
Pacific Reporter	P.	Alaska, Arizona, California, Colorado, Hawai'i, Idaho, Kansas, Montana, Nevada, New Mexico, Oklahoma, Oregon, Utah, Washington & Wyoming
	P.2d	
	P.3d	
South Eastern Reporter	S.E.	Georgia, North Carolina, South Carolina, Virginia & West Virginia
	S.E.2d	

South Western Reporter	S.W.	Arkansas, Kentucky, Missouri, Tennessee & Texas
	S.W.2d	
	S.W.3d	
Southern Reporter	So.	Alabama, Florida, Louisiana & Mississippi
	So. 2d	
	So. 3d	

Georgia trial court opinions are not published in any reporter but researchers may be able to locate these decisions through contacting the applicable clerk of court, consulting court websites, and both Lexis and Westlaw provide access to selected Georgia trial court opinions.

E. Federal Judicial Opinions

Federal Judicial opinions are divided into different reporters by level of courts as set forth in Table 6-2.

Table 6-2. Publication of Federal Judicial Opinions

Federal Court	Reporter and Publisher	Reporter Abbreviation
United States Supreme Court	*United States Reports* (U.S. Govt)	U.S.
	Supreme Court Reporter (West)	S. Ct.
	United States Supreme Court Reports, Lawyer's Edition (Lexis)	L. Ed. L. Ed. 2d
United States Courts of Appeals (all circuits)	*Federal Reporter* (Published opinions) (West)	F. F.2d F.3d
	Federal Appendix (Unpublished opinions) (West) (publication ceased in 2021)	Fed. Appx.
United States District Courts	*Federal Supplement* (West)	F. Supp. F. Supp. 2d
	Federal Rules Decisions (Federal Procedural Rules) (West)	F.R.D.

The United States Supreme Court's opinions are published in three different reporters. *United States Reports*, is the official reporter and is published by the U.S. Government Publishing Office. The Reporter of Decisions includes a syllabus prior to each decision in the official reporter. The syllabus is an editorial enhancement that should not be cited in legal filings. The *Supreme Court Reporter* published by West, contains the editorial enhancements created by West editors; and the *United States Supreme Court Reports, Lawyer's Edition* contains the editorial enhancements added by Lexis editors.

All reported decisions of the thirteen circuit federal appellate courts are unofficially published in the *Federal Reporter* produced by West. The *Federal Reporter* will contain the text of the federal appellate court opinions along with editorial enhancements selected by West editors. West also published the *Federal Appendix*, an unofficial reporter containing selected unpublished and editorially enhanced decisions of the federal appellate courts.

United States federal district court decisions that judges select for publication are published by West in the *Federal Supplement*, which includes the West editors' editorial enhancements. West produces the *Federal Rules Decisions* reporter that includes federal district court cases on federal civil and criminal procedure. Both of these publications include decisions from all federal district courts.

Opinions from the United States Supreme Court can be located online at the Supreme Court website.[9] Selected opinions from the United States Court of Appeals and federal district courts going back to April of 2004 are provided online by the United States Government Publishing Office at govinfo. gov.

F. Parts of an Opinion

Researchers need to understand the parts of an opinion to efficiently analyze an opinion and cite it correctly. Below are descriptions of the various parts of a case depicted in Figure 6-1.

i. Case Citation

The case citation indicates which regional reporter a state judicial opinion is located in, as well as the official state reporter if one is published. These two

---

9. Supreme Court of the United States, https://www.supremecourt.gov/ [https://perma.cc/3P55-BDG8].

Figure 6-1. Parts of an Opinion[10]

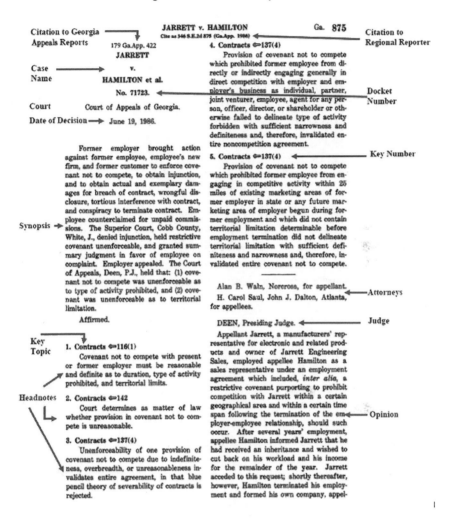

10. Image of case, published originally in the *South Eastern Reporter 2d*, used with permission from Thomson Reuters.

citations together are called the *parallel citation* to a case. When it is a federal court opinion, the citation will refer to the applicable federal reporter.

ii. Case Name

This includes the names of each party. At trial court, the plaintiff(s) are always listed first followed by the defendant(s). In an appellate court (intermediate or last resort), the first party is the party that is appealing the previous decision, whether it is appealing the trial court decision or the intermediate court decision. The party appealing the decision is called the appellant and the party responding to the appeal is called the appellee.

iii. Docket Number

This is the number that the clerk of the court gives a case to make it easily identifiable. The docket number is used to retrieve records related to the case, and all actions in a case are recorded in order of occurrence in the docket. When a case is appealed, a new docket number is issued by the appellate court. Typically docket numbers begin with the designation of the year the matter was initiated with the court.

iv. Court

The court that issued the decision.

v. Date of Decision

The day the court issued its decision. Sometimes you will see the date the court conducted a hearing on the legal matter, but researchers should use the date the court issued the decision for citation purposes.

vi. Synopsis

This is a summary of the case by the editors of the reporter. This typically includes the basic background of the case, the judge that wrote the opinion, as well as the court's holdings. This can be used by researchers to quickly evaluate whether cases are relevant to their legal issue. This is not part of the judicial opinion drafted by the court and should not be cited by researchers. Researchers should cite only to the text of the opinion issued by the court.

vii. Headnotes, Topics, and Key Numbers

Chapter 7 discusses how researchers can use headnotes, topics and key numbers in detail. Essentially these are tools that assist researchers in locating cases relevant to their legal issue. Headnotes summarize the points of law that editors identified in cases. West editors then assign these points of law into categories and subcategories, known as topics and key numbers, for classification according to the West Digest System described in Chapter 7. Topics and key numbers are consistent across jurisdictions and are updated over time.

Lexis includes headnotes and topics for United States Supreme Court decisions published in its *United States Supreme Court Reports, Lawyer's Edition* in print and online.

Opinions issued in official reporters usually will not contain synopses, headnotes, topics or key numbers, but they will contain the other parts of the opinion.

viii. Attorneys

Immediately preceding the text of the court's opinion, the decision lists the names of the attorneys of record representing the parties and their firms.

ix. Opinion

The actual text of the decision is the referred to as the opinion. A majority opinion is the opinion written by the majority of judges agreeing on the opinion. A concurring opinion is the opinion of judges that agree with the outcome of the decision but differ on the legal analysis of the majority decision. Lastly, a dissenting opinion is an opinion written by judges that disagree with the outcome of the decision. Please note that only majority opinions will be considered precedent for future decisions but concurring and dissenting opinions can provide valuable insights on a legal issue.

G. Citation of Cases

Scholarly writing follows the citation rules included in *The Bluebook* or *Association of Legal Writing Directors Guide to Legal Citation* (ALWD). Rules for citation to cases are set forth in Rule 10 of *The Bluebook* and Rule/Chapter 12 of ALWD.

For documents submitted in Georgia Courts, researchers need to comply with the rules issued by the Court of Appeals of Georgia and the Supreme Court of Georgia.[11] Georgia Supreme Court Rule 22 provides that "Georgia citations must include the volume and page number of the official Georgia reporters."[12] When researchers cite to these official reporters of Georgia it is often common practice to include a parallel citation to the regional reporter so that all researchers can locate the case through the Georgia reporters or through the regional reporters. Here is an example of a citation of a case with a parallel citation: *Watson v. Waffle House, Inc.*, 253 Ga. 671, 324 S.E.2d 175 (1985).

Citations to judicial opinions of another state will not contain the parallel citation. These citations will refer only to the regional reporter: *Miller Mech., Inc. v. Ruth*, 300 So. 2d 11 (Fla. 1974). Note, when a citation does not contain a parallel citation, the parenthetical must indicate the court that issued the decision, as set forth in Table 1.3 of *The Bluebook*.

A researcher must also understand the elements of case citations in order to efficiently research. Table 6-3 lists the elements of a case citation. When researching secondary sources, statutes, cases or other legal materials, researchers will see a citation to a case formatted similar to this:

Glisson v. Glob. Sec. Servs., LLC, 287 Ga. App. 640, 653 S.E.2d 85 (2007).

Table 6-3. Elements of a Case Citation

| Parties | Volume Number | Official Reporter | Starting Page | Parallel Citation | | | Year of Decision |
				Volume Number	Regional Reporter	Starting Page	
Glisson v. Glob. Sec. Servs., LLC	287	Ga. App.	640	653	S.E.2d	85	2007

---

11. Ga. Ct. App R. 24.
12. Ga. Sup. Ct. R. 22.

Parties: This first part of a citation includes the first party listed as a plaintiff (or appellant) and the first defendant or (appellee). There certainly could be additional parties as part of the legal dispute, but *The Bluebook* Rule 10 only requires the first party listed to be included in the citation. Consult Tables 6 and 13 for abbreviations that may be commonly used in party names, such as Bros. for Brothers.

Volume Number: The first number in the citation refers to the volume number. In this instance, the case is located in volume 287 of *Georgia Appeals Reports*.

Official Reporter: This refers to the official reporter where the case is located, *Georgia Appeals Reports*. Table 1.3 in *The Bluebook* to lists the reporter abbreviations by jurisdiction.

Starting Page: This number is the starting page of the opinion within the applicable volume. In this example, the case will start on page 640 of volume 287 in *Georgia Appeals Reports*. Sometimes researchers will see a citation similar to this: *Glisson v. Glob. Sec. Servs., LLC*, 287 Ga. App. 640, 642, 653 S.E.2d 85, 87 (2007).

This citation includes a *pinpoint citation* or *pin cite*, which are the numbers following the starting page (642 and 87). This pin cite is included as a part of the citation when the individual is referring to a specific part of a case and wants to refer the reader to the specific page on which a cited quotation appears. In this example, the citation refers the reader to page 642 of volume 287 in *Georgia Appeals Reports* and to page 87 of volume 653 of the *South Eastern Reporter 2d*.

Parallel Citation: A citation may contain a parallel citation. This citation indicates that this case is in both the *Georgia Appeals Reports* and the *South Eastern Reporter 2d* in the volumes and page number displayed in the citation.

Year of Decision: This is the year that the court issued its decision.

III. Locating Judicial Opinions

There are five major ways to locate relevant Georgia state court decisions or federal court decisions. Researchers can locate cases by consulting secondary sources and reviewing the cases cited in those secondary sources. Researchers can consult statutes and find case citations included in either annotations or citator reports for the statutes. Researchers can search in online sources ranging from Google Scholar to premium databases. Finally, researchers can use citators and digest systems, such as West's Analysis of American Law, to locate cases. These approaches to research are described below.

A. Secondary Sources

One of the best ways to find relevant cases is to use secondary sources. Secondary sources explain or describe the law, and they provide citations to key cases on a legal topic or issue. Researchers can then use the citations to find applicable cases.

B. Statutory Annotations

Another good way to locate applicable cases is by using the case annotations of a statutory code. Case annotations are cases selected by the editors of a commercial publisher of a statutory code that interpret the statutes. These annotations will be organized topically in print versions of the code and are also included on Lexis and Westlaw. Review Chapter 5 for more information on locating cases in statutory case annotations.

C. Online Databases

While researchers can use print versions of the reporters for case research, case research is much more efficient if it is conducted online. Fastcase, Lexis, and Westlaw all permit researchers to research Georgia state court, and applicable federal court opinions online. Researchers may use keyword or terms and connector searching within these databases to locate relevant cases. Each database has its own *syntax*, or rules, for creating terms and connector searches, so researchers will need to review the different ways they can search for exact phrases, proximity between terms, use root expanders, and other terms and connector features within each database.

Another option for researching cases online is to search within specific parts of cases. Lexis and Westlaw each provide researchers with an "advance search" option, and on Lexis researchers can limit their search by segment, while on Westlaw researchers can limit their search by fields. When selecting these options, researchers limit the search to the specific parts of a case which coincide with the different parts of judicial opinions discussed above. Researches will be able to search the parties, judge, headnotes, topics, synopses, and other fields. This enables researchers to focus their search to locate opinions on a particular legal issue or topic, written by a specific judge, or involving a precise set of facts. Each database provides a list and description of the different segments or fields that researchers are able to search.

D. Citators

In addition to ensuring that a case is still good law, which is discussed below in Chapter 11, citators permit researchers to locate other applicable cases and primary law, and secondary sources. Having found a relevant case, researchers can use citators to find other relevant cases. Authority Check in Fastcase, Shepard's in Lexis, and KeyCite in Westlaw expand case research and assist the researcher in validating cases.

Each citator has different filters to narrow the cases that cited to the original case. Shepard's and KeyCite enable researchers to filter by jurisdiction, headnote, depth of treatment or discussion, reported status, and as well as other filters. Shepard's and KeyCite provide citations to other primary and secondary materials that cite to cases, which researchers can then use to expand their searches for additional relevant primary and secondary sources. Fastcase's Authority Check provides researchers with a list of cases citing to the relevant case, along with the ability to filter the results by jurisdiction.

E. Headnotes

Researchers can use the headnotes in Westlaw or Lexis to locate additional cases for the point of law in the applicable headnote. This can be a very efficient way to find other cases applicable to a legal issue and is fully described in Chapter 7.

IV. Validating Cases

Researchers need to validate cases to ensure that the cases they want to rely on remain good law. Shepard's, KeyCite, and the Bad Law Bot on Fastcase include signals indicating negative treatment to cases available in their premium databases. However, a citator's warning that a case may no longer be good law may be limited to only one part of a case. To determine what part or parts of the case have been invalidated, the researcher needs to evaluate the cases carefully. The process of evaluating cases to assure that the law remains valid is described in Chapter 11.

V. Reading Cases

Once researchers have located a potentially relevant case, there are tools to efficiently read cases. Researchers should first read the synopsis and headnotes. These will quickly alert researchers to whether a case may be on-point for the legal issue. Researchers also can use the headnote to jump directly to the portion of the opinion dealing with a headnote that is relevant to their legal issue.

If researchers determine that a case may be relevant based upon the synopsis and headnotes, then they should slowly read the case, take notes, and organize the cases, as set forth in Chapter 2.

VI. Conclusion

When locating cases, researchers need to find binding cases within the proper jurisdiction that are published. There are different approaches that researchers can take to find these cases, and they should select the most efficient one depending on the type of research project.

Chapter 7

Researching Judicial Opinions

After reading this chapter, you will be able to:

- Describe the relationship between case headnotes and digests;

- Explain how West's digests function as an index for finding cases across jurisdictions;

- List strategies for using West's topic and key numbers system to find cases online; and

- Find cases using West's topic and key numbers system.

Researchers may use Georgia cases to learn more about how regulations, statutes, and the Georgia constitution have been applied in particular cases. However, when there are no statutes governing in an area of law, the area is said to be governed by *common law*. Consequently, cases are important for researchers in understanding both statutory and common law.

Researchers may find cases by starting from primary sources such as statutes, as described in Chapter 5. Or researchers may find cases starting from secondary sources such as legal encyclopedias, periodicals, treatises, or *American Law Reports*, as described in Chapter 4, or by conducting keyword and advanced searches explained in Chapters 3 and 6. Another approach is to consult a digest system, such as West's topic and key numbers system to find cases. Using the digest system to find cases is the focus of this chapter.

I. Case Headnotes and Digests

West created an organizational system that helps researchers find cases that is called the digest system. The digest system is helpful for researchers and attorneys because it makes it easier to find relevant law, and it can help researchers focus on important aspects within individual cases. Other legal publishers, such as Lexis, provide access to their own digest systems. Researchers can use Lexis's system in much the same way as they would use the West digest system as described below.

A. What Is the West Digest System?

The *digest system* is an organizational tool that helps researchers identify cases addressing particular issues of law; and points of law from cases are organized by legal issue. The digest system works because it is comprehensive, and it is organized consistently across jurisdictions. It is comprehensive because it contains all the points of law that West editors identify in the cases published by West in its reporters. The points of law identified in cases are called *headnotes*.

Figure 7.1 shows the first page of an opinion published in a West reporter. In the Figure, the headnotes are numbered, reflecting the order in which they appear in the case.

In the West digest system, each headnote is assigned to the digest topic and key number that correspond with the points of law contained in each headnote. Some headnotes may be assigned to two topics and key numbers, or to two key numbers in the same topic, if the headnote combines points of law. These topics and key numbers are the tools that researchers use to identify every case that has addressed the point of law which is *classified*, or organized and assigned, to a particular topic and key number.

In order to use the digest system, a researcher needs to know both the topic and the key number for a point of law, in the same way as one needs to know both the X-axis and the Y-axis coordinates in order to identify a point in a graph. In Figure 7.1, after each headnote number, the topic and key number are listed. Headnote number one reflects the topic Landlord and Tenant, while headnote number two reflects the topic Negligence. Headnote one has the key number 167(8), while headnote number two has the key number 1037(4).

Figure 7-1. First Page of An Opinion from West's *South Eastern Reports*[1]

SPEAR v. CALHOUN   Ga. **71**
Cite as 584 S.E.2d 71 (Ga.App. 2003)

the convictions did not merge.[25]

Judgment affirmed.

BLACKBURN, P.J., and ELLINGTON, J., concur.

261 Ga.App. 835

SPEAR et al.

v.

CALHOUN et al.

No. A03A0392.

Court of Appeals of Georgia.

June 20, 2003.

Mother of victim who was killed in accidental shooting brought wrongful death action against owner of apartment complex where shooting occurred. The State Court, Fulton County, Brogdon, J., granted summary judgment in favor of property owner, and mother appealed. The Court of Appeals, Smith, C.J., held that property owner did not breach duty not to injure accidental shooting victim wilfully and wantonly.

Affirmed.

1. Landlord and Tenant ☞167(8)

Owner of apartment complex did not breach duty not to injure accidental shooting victim, who was, at most, a social guest or licensee, wilfully and wantonly, where property owner did not have any knowledge about actual danger of firearms being discharged by revelers on New Year's Eve at or

near his property. West's Ga.Code Ann. § 51–3–2(b).

2. Negligence ☞1037(4)

As a general rule, the owner or occupier of land is liable to invitees for injuries caused by his failure to exercise ordinary care in keeping his premises and approaches safe. West's Ga.Code Ann. § 51–3–1.

3. Negligence ☞1037(4), 1040(4)

Liability for an injury to an invitee is predicated upon the landowner's or proprietor's superior knowledge of a hazard or dangerous condition existing on his premises that may subject an invitee to an unreasonable risk of harm; but when the person on the premises is merely a social guest, owner of the premises is liable to a licensee only for willful or wanton injury. West's Ga.Code Ann. §§ 51–3–1, 51–3–2(b).

4. Negligence ☞210

Regardless of the age or capacity of the injured or deceased person, in the absence of a breach of some legal duty toward such person by the defendant, there can be no liability.

5. Landlord and Tenant ☞167(8)

Since shooting victim was, at most, a social guest or licensee, owner of apartment complex owed only the duty not to injure her wilfully and wantonly, as no evidence indicated victim was on the premises at the invitation of one of owner's tenants.

6. Negligence ☞275

The standard of "wilful or wanton" imports deliberate acts or omissions, or such conduct as which discloses an inference of conscious indifference to consequences.

See publication Words and Phrases for other judicial constructions and definitions.

---

1. *Spear v. Calhoun*, 584 S.E.2d 71 (Ga.App. 2003). Used with the permission of Thomson Reuters.

Cases address a wide variety of legal issues. There are around 400 topics in the West's digest system. West makes a full list of the topics available online in their Westlaw and Westlaw Campus Research products, as seen in Figure 7.2 and in multiple print products including *West's Analysis of American Law*. The Westlaw Campus Research platform is currently available on Georgia college and university campuses through the Georgia Library Learning Online (GALILEO) service operated by the University System of Georgia. To use West's digest system on Westlaw Campus Research, users need to click first on the "Tools" link and then "West Key Number System."

Figure 7-2. Topics List from West's Digest System[2]

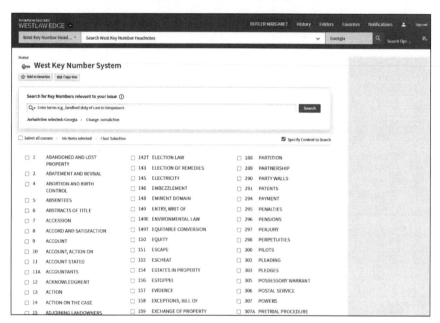

---

2. Used with permission of Thomson Reuters.

Figure 7.3 shows the list of topics on Lexis. The digest available on Lexis offers many similar functions to the digest available through West. Other vendors' digest systems may be specialized and cover only particular kinds of cases or issues, such as the subject-focused United States Patent Quarterly Classification Outline which includes intellectual property cases.[3]

Figure 7-3. Topics List from Lexis[4]

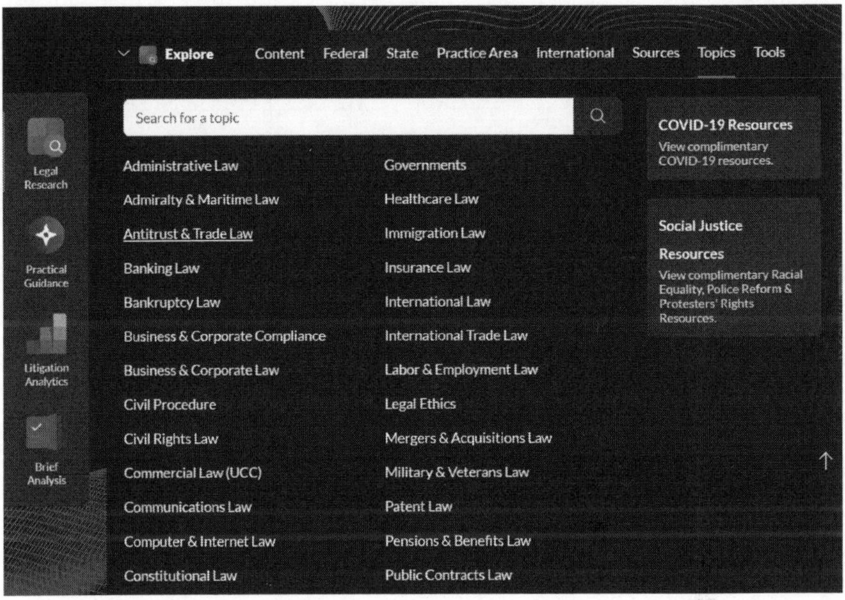

The West digest system is comprehensive because it contains points of law from all published cases. *Digests* are the multi-volume sets of *headnotes*, or points of law from cases, that are organized by topic and published with a jurisdictional focus. For example, the *Georgia Digest, 2d.*, contains all of the headnotes from Georgia cases published by West since 1942. Headnotes from earlier published Georgia cases were published in the *Georgia Digest*. The

---

3. BloombergLaw, *Product Health & Walkthrough: Headnotes and Classification Outlines, https://bltx-help.bloombergtax.com/docs/blt-060-cases-and-court-rules.html #headnotes-and-classification-outlines* [https://perma.cc/KE9M-VYL7].

4. Used with permission of LexisNexis.

Federal Practice Digest contains only headnotes from federal court opinions, while the *Decennial Digest* contains headnotes from state and federal court cases which have been published in West's National Reporter System.

In print, the digest volumes are all organized the same way, according to the topics listed in *West's Analysis of American Law*. That means that a topic and key number from a case in one jurisdiction, such as Florida, may be used to find Georgia cases on the same legal issue. Although some topics have been renamed or reorganized as the law has changed and time has passed, the digest is organized to make it easy for researchers to find all the cases over time. There are conversion tables in print, and cross-references online, which enable researchers to find all the headnotes that have ever been classified to a current or an obsolete topic and key number.

The easiest way to use the digest system is online through Westlaw or Westlaw Campus Research (a similar research product), if that is available through the researcher's institution. Print digests that include Georgia or federal cases are found in the *Georgia Digest* (Georgia cases only), *South Eastern Digest* (Georgia cases only), *Federal Practice Digest* (federal cases only), and *Decennial Digest* (state and federal cases). As print reporters and digests have become more expensive, libraries have made budget choices to make online access to these resources rather than continuing to pay increasing costs for subscriptions to print digests and case reporters. As a result, this chapter focuses on strategies for using the online digest to locate relevant cases.

B. Consider Jurisdiction Before Searching

The scope of most digests is based on jurisdiction, as noted above. There are also topical digests, such as West's *Education Law Digest*. Searching efficiently requires that the researcher identify the controlling jurisdiction for the research project. If you are researching Georgia law, you would want to make sure that your search is set to only provide Georgia materials. You will have the choice to search for only state materials, or only federal materials from the jurisdiction of Georgia, or both the federal and state materials of Georgia.

II. Strategies for Using the Digests

As you research, your path will be determined in part by the information you have already gathered. Following are a variety of strategies that a researcher may try using West's digests. These approaches often have analogous approaches with other research platforms' digest systems, such as the "Topics" tab on Lexis's research platform. The strategies described here will likely continue to be possible, even as the online platforms may change the appearance of their research systems. Understanding how the strategies work makes it much easier to figure out how to apply the strategy when a system's interface changes. The strategies described are the "One Good Case" Method, searching using West's Key Number Headnotes tool, browsing by topic, searching West's Topics & Key Numbers list (the virtual digest), and searching on Westlaw using topics and key numbers as search terms.

A. The "One Good Case" Method

There are many reasons why a researcher may have one good case when beginning their case research. Perhaps you found a citation in a secondary source footnote. A colleague may have recommended one good case. The first step in this method would be to review the "good case" in Westlaw. The case will include a list of headnotes before the body of the opinion. By skimming the summary of the case and the headnotes, you can quickly identify the part(s) of the case actually addressing your legal issue.

In the online version of the one good case method, researchers can click on the topic and key number combination to retrieve all the cases that include a headnote that has been classified to that topic and key number. This allows researchers to expand their research to and locate additional on-point cases. If you consult Figure 7.4, you will see that the topic and key number combination for the first headnote is 233k1341. The topic Landlord and Tenant is represented by 233, and the legal issue within that topic is represented by the key number 1341. The hyperlink combination 233k1341, if selected, would retrieve every case within the selected jurisdiction that includes a headnote with that topic and key number.

Figure 7-4. Online View of Topic and Key Number Showing Hierarchy[5]

	Landlord and Tenant	🗝	
1	Owner of apartment complex did not breach duty not to injure accidental shooting victim, who was, at most, a social guest or licensee, wilfully and wantonly, where property owner did not have any knowledge about actual danger of firearms being discharged by revelers on New Year's Eve at or near his property. West's Ga.Code Ann. § 51–3–2(b).	233	Landlord and Tenant
		233V	Enjoyment and Use of Premises
		233V(J)	Liability for Dangerous or Defective Conditions
	1 Case that cites this headnote	233V(J)8	Defenses and Mitigating Circumstances
		233k1341	Notice to or knowledge of injured party as to defects
		(Formerly 233k167(8))	
2	**Negligence**	🗝	
	As a general rule, the owner or occupier of land is liable to invitees for injuries caused by his failure to exercise ordinary care in keeping his premises and approaches safe. West's Ga.Code Ann. § 51–3–1.	272	Negligence
		272XVII	Premises Liability
		272XVII(C)	Standard of Care
		272k1034	Status of Entrant
		272k1037	Invitees
		272k1037(4)	Care required in general

The results of selecting that topic and key number are shown in Figure 7.5. The outline organization showing at the top of this results list mirrors the listing of the topic and key number as shown in the case. There are 29 Georgia headnotes that have been classified to this key number in the topic Landlord and Tenant. There will be no more than 29 cases included in this list, and there may be fewer. If a single case had multiple headnotes assigned to the topic Landlord and key number 1341, the total number of cases would be smaller than the total number of headnotes.

---

5. Used with permission of Thomson Reuters.

If you were interested in learning more about the other defenses or mitigating circumstances that may be available for landlords in claims of dangerous or defective conditions by tenants, you could click on 233V(J)8, which is one level up from the key number in the outline shown in Figure 7.5. As displayed in Figure 7.5, the results would include 242 Georgia headnotes. However, clicking on other lines in the outline might not be as useful, given the thousands of headnotes that would be retrieved.

Figure 7-5. Headnotes from Georgia Case Classified to 233k1341, Landlord and Tenant Key Number 1341[6]

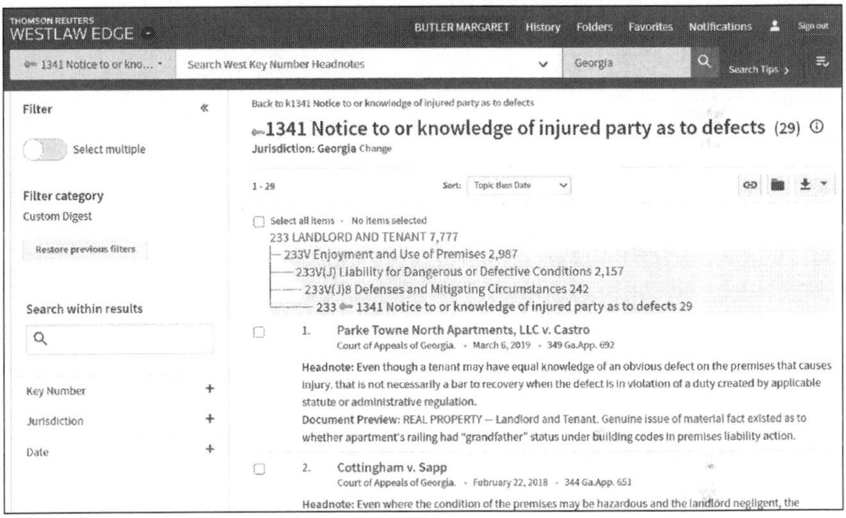

B. Search Using West Key Number Headnotes Tool

West's digest system gathers all the headnotes, or points of law, from all the cases that are published by West. West adds headnotes and other editorial enhancements to cases that courts have not designated as published, as does Lexis. The Search West Key Number Headnotes tool allows researchers to search through all of those headnotes by keyword or to filter their search results by particular topic.

---

6. Used with permission of Thomson Reuters.

A researcher may search headnotes by keyword or by terms and connectors to find all the headnotes on a specific legal issue. Once the headnotes are identified as relevant, the researcher would then consult those relevant cases. Researchers may also find it useful to note any relevant topics and key numbers, as they may be used to expand the search.

Researchers may want to search the digest, or headnotes from all cases, rather than simply searching all cases themselves. The first reason is that West headnotes are rich with search terms. Headnotes also typically include citations to relevant statutes, acronyms in both abbreviated and spelled out forms, and briefly state the point of law. Also, by searching headnotes the researcher can more quickly identify whether the legal issue assigned to a topic and key number would be of use in answering the relevant legal question. When searching cases instead, researchers would have to look more closely at individual cases to determine whether they are relevant to the research question.

The researcher generates the keyword search as discussed in Chapter 3. The search can be either a natural language search or a terms and connectors search. A natural language search is limited to 100 results, while a terms and connectors search will retrieve as many results as the search identifies. Figure 7.6 illustrates the natural language search "motorist and vehicle," which retrieves 100 results. Figure 7.7 shows the terms and connectors search "motorist /s vehicle," which retrieves over 1,500 topic and key number combinations. Terms and connector searching is recommended if the terms are more unique, though a large set of terms and connectors results may be effectively filtered by additional keyword searching.

Figure 7-6. Results of Natural Language Search from Search West Key Number Headnotes Tool[7]

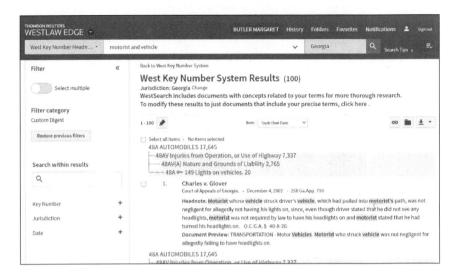

Figure 7-7. Results of Terms and Connectors Search from Search West Key Number Headnotes Tool[8]

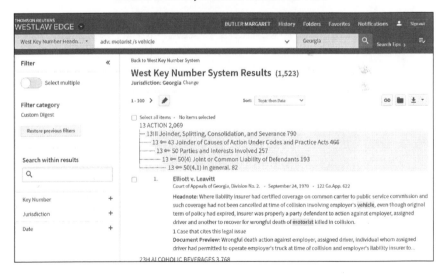

---

7. Used with permission of Thomson Reuters.
8. Used with permission of Thomson Reuters.

The results of natural language and terms and connectors West Key Number Headnotes search, shown in Figures 7.6 and 7.7, are called *custom digests*. The natural language search retrieves a maximum of 100 key numbers, and the results appear in alphabetical order by topic. The easiest way to browse this type of custom digest, to see which topics and key numbers are likely responsive to the search query, is to open the Key Number filter. That shows the researcher a list of the topics included in the results, as well as the number of headnotes assigned to each topic. The researcher can then consider the topics listed and identify the topic and key numbers that may be helpful or relevant for the legal issue being researched.

After identifying a single topic for further analysis, researchers can easily search within that topic for headnotes containing particular keywords. Figure 7.8 shows the beginning of the outline for the topic Postal Service. To search the entire topic, add keywords or terms and connectors to the Westlaw search box above the outline. The search bar includes the scope of the search, showing the topic 306 Postal Service to the left of the search box. To search specific lines within the topic, check the boxes next to the lines and then run a search in the search box.

Figure 7-8. Searching Within a Single Topic[9]

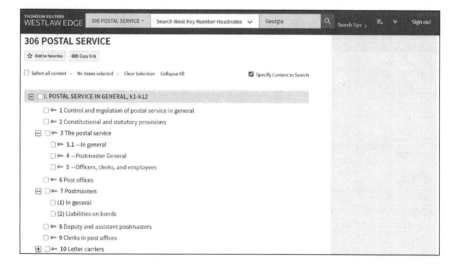

---

9. Used with permission of Thomson Reuters.

Once a researcher has identified a topic and key number, the researcher can review all the headnotes assigned to that particular key number. Considerations at that point include not only the legal substance of the headnote, but also how recently the case was decided, how many other cases have cited to the judicial opinion corresponding to the headnote, and whether the case itself has been negatively treated in a subsequent case.

C. Search West's Topics & Key Numbers List

Another strategy for finding helpful topics and key numbers involves searching West's Topics & Key Numbers page. You can use the "Search for Key Numbers relevant to your issue" tool to identify useful topic and key number combinations. The results list will include hyperlinks directly to the collection of headnotes reflecting your issue of law. Figure 7.9 illustrates results of searching for life estates remainderman interest.

Figure 7-9. Results of Using Search for Key Numbers Relevant To Your Issue Tool[10]

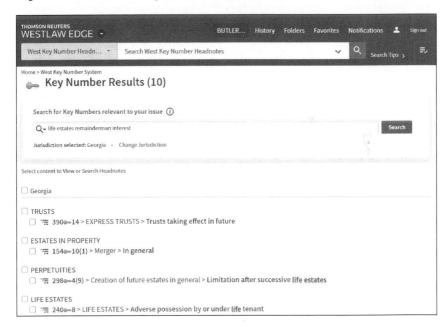

---

10. Used with permission of Thomson Reuters.

Another way to find potentially useful topics and key numbers is by searching from the Westlaw home screen and reviewing the Overview results section called Key Numbers—Points of Law Found in Cases. See Figure 7.10. These two tools for identifying topics and key numbers do not always provide identical results, so it is worth checking both places.

Figure 7-10. Key Numbers – Points of Law Found in Cases from Westlaw Search Overview[11]

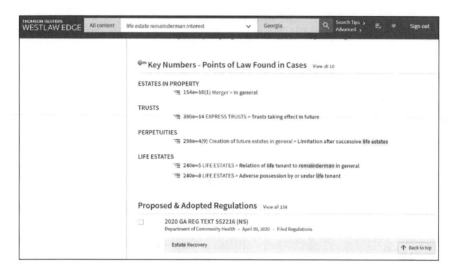

The hyperlinked lists of suggested topics and key numbers shown in Figures 7.9 and Figures 7.10 include an outline icon. Hovering over this icon shows the key number hierarchy, or outline for the topic. This information is useful in determining whether a recommended topic and key number are worth investigating further or may be disregarded as irrelevant.

As in other approaches, once a topic and key number are identified as relevant, researchers review the headnotes to cases with those topic and key number assignments and identify which cases to evaluate further in their research.

---

11. Used with permission of Thomson Reuters.

D. Browse by Topic

Researchers may browse the list of topics and key numbers as a starting point in their research. They may also browse the outline of a known topic to identify additional relevant key numbers from the topic.

The Topics and Key Numbers page provides researchers the ability to browse, although browsing is not generally recommended if you are unfamiliar with the legal subject. The list of topics is in alphabetical order, and each topic has a corresponding information icon available if you hover over the topic with your mouse. This information is worth the time it takes to review, as it includes an explanation of the topic's scope.

The scope information for topics refers to a list of subjects that are included in the topic, as well as a list of subjects that are excluded. For subjects that are excluded, researchers are guided to potentially relevant topics. For example, a researcher hoping to learn more about the law governing the licensure of aircraft pilots may skim the list of topics and select "Pilots." However, the scope information for that topic indicates that the information in this topic is limited to riverboat pilots. The licensure of aircraft pilots is excluded and covered instead in the topic Aviation.

Whether you find a helpful topic and key number by browsing the topic list or you found a topic and key number in another source, it can be helpful to browse the key numbers that are nearby the relevant topic and key number. Each topic is organized in an outline structure and may be viewed by expanding the topic on Westlaw.

The topic Postal Service is shown in Figure 7.8. If a legal issue related to the status of an employee as a postal clerk arose, it is not immediately clear whether a researcher should consult key number 5, which includes points of law related to officers, clerks, and employees, or key number 9, which includes points of law related to clerks in post offices. In situations like this, it may be helpful to check both places. Also, headnotes stating a rule may be classified to one line, while headnotes stating the burden of proof associated with the rule may be in a different line in the same topic. Thus, an attorney may find it useful to browse nearby a known topic and key number. This is another example of how it can be useful to check the neighborhood nearby a relevant source to see whether additional helpful information or sources can be found.

E. Use West Topics and Key Numbers as Search Terms

West topics and key numbers can be used as search terms when searching for other materials available in Westlaw. There are a few things to know to make this work. First, you need to know how to format your search query. Second, you need to know how to search for topics and key numbers that may have changed over time.

The structure for creating a topic and key number search is to use the number associated with a topic, followed by the letter "k," followed by the line of the key number hierarchy. Some topics are numbers, such as Postal Service 306. Other topics are numbers followed by letters, such as Election Law with the topic number 142T. The researcher can tell from the letter at the end of the topic that the topic was created after the original outline.

When a key number hierarchy is shown, such as when conducting a digest search through all the West headnotes or when viewing headnotes in a case, the key number to use in constructing the search is the bottom-most line in the hierarchy. It will provide the most specific, hopefully on-point, results. Again, looking at Figure 7.8, the search 306k13 would retrieve all the headnotes in the jurisdiction selected related to "mailable matter in general" that are found in the topic of the Postal Service. This key number would be useful for identifying whether a particular item, such as chickens, are eligible for being mailed. There should be no spaces included between the topic and key number.

Topics and key numbers are updated from time to time. This may happen when an area of law develops, and consequently additional lines are added to a topic. It may also happen as language of the law changes. When these changes happen, you may encounter a phrase such as "formerly 233k167(8)" below the topic and key number combination for a headnote. Figure 7.11 shows that the topic of Landlord and Tenant has been re-numbered to make it more helpful to researchers. The topic being searched is represented by the number 233 and the key number is 167(8). Figure 7.11 shows a topic and key number search and its results, limited to the jurisdiction of Georgia.

Figure 7-11. Topic and Key Number Search and Results[12]

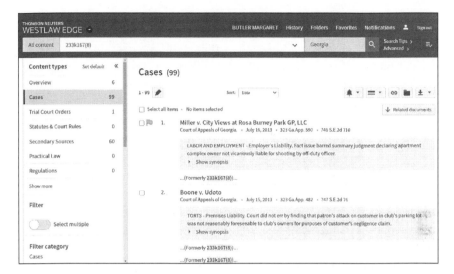

However, West includes obsolete topic and key number combinations in the classification information for all reclassified headnotes. By including the "formerly 233k167(8)" language researchers are able to retrieve headnotes that were originally assigned to that topic and key number but have since been updated to either a new topic and new key number, or a new key number within the same topic. A search for the obsolete topic and key number combination will retrieve any case that was formerly assigned to the topic and key number, searched even if those headnotes have been updated to reflect the updated topic and key number classification.

If you are starting your research with a former topic and key number, and you want to make sure you are also retrieving all relevant recent cases, the best approach is straightforward. Run a topic and key number search of the former topic and key number. Review the results and identify a case that looks on point with the issue you are researching. You will see an updated topic and key number associated with the headnote in addition to the "formerly" designation. Simply search the new topic and key number and you will retrieve the more recent headnotes.

---

12. Used with permission of Thomson Reuters.

III. Efficiently Navigating a Case Using the Headnotes

Once you have identified headnotes that are of interest, you will want to review the cases from which they came. This section will explain how to use the headnote to navigate the case. This guidance is applicable whether you are researching in Westlaw or using other online digest systems.

A. Using the Headnotes

You may skim the headnotes to see if the case addresses issues of interest to you or relevant to your legal issue. You may use the headnotes to quickly locate the part of the opinion that addresses the legal issue of interest. When researching online, headnote numbers link the reader between the headnote and the part of the case where the discussion of that issue of law begins.

B. Reading the Case

Researchers should read and consider cases fully before relying on them whether in scholarship or before a court. Although the headnotes may direct you to the part of the case that is most relevant, other aspects of the case provide additional context and will guide the researcher in analyzing the case.

IV. Conclusion

Headnote and digest systems are very valuable to researchers. The points of law in cases, identified as headnotes and categorized in digests by legal issue, help researchers find all cases in a jurisdiction that address a particular issue of law. Strategies for using digests include starting with a known topic and key number, browsing by topic, and using the topic and key number as search terms. Although the headnotes make it easier for researchers to focus on particular parts of a case, researchers should read cases fully before relying on them.

Chapter 8

Administrative Law

After reading this chapter you will be able to:

- List the steps for consulting Georgia regulations;
- Describe the differences between Georgia agency rules and decisions;
- Locate Georgia agency rules and decisions;
- List the steps for federal administrative research;
- Explain the documents from state and federal administrative branches that mirror each other; and
- Explain that the agency itself may be the best source of information.

I. Introduction to Administrative Law

Legislatures pass legislation called organic laws that create governmental agencies. Agencies may also be created by executive order, but that is relatively rare. Legislatures pass enabling statutes to authorize governmental agencies to carry out functions that require attention and expertise beyond that of the legislature. These government functions include assuring the health and welfare of vulnerable citizens, such as through food and health-care programs; assuring public safety through the implementation and enforcement of licensing standards in a variety of professions; and similar functions. Typically, legislatures enact laws addressing large scale concerns and then agencies promulgate and enforce regulations in furtherance of the legislature's goals. Agencies are especially important in areas requiring ongoing and specialized knowledge, such as where scientific or technical expertise is needed or when professional licensing standards are being maintained.

Enabling legislation sets out the scope of the agency's authority and power. Agency powers mirror those of the three branches of federal government. They include rule making (quasi-legislative power), administrative adjudication (quasi-judicial power), and enforcement (quasi-executive power). In Georgia, governmental agencies usually are required to follow the operational rules set out in the Georgia Administrative Procedure Act[1] when exercising agency powers. Agencies promulgate rules, which have the force of law and are primary sources in legal research, issue rulings, and make determinations about license or permit applications. Agencies may also produce other documents helpful to a researcher. These documents include agency guidance and interpretations.

II. Georgia Administrative Rules

Rules, also called regulations, are promulgated by administrative agencies. Administrative rules may initially appear similar to statutes in their structure or format, but there is an important difference. Generally, statutes provide broad guidance regarding the law and legislative intention, while regulations provide detailed guidance that carries out legislative intent. The broad statements of the legislative goals that guide the agency may be found in the organic and enabling legislation. The legislature authorizes the agency to promulgate regulations in fulfillment of the legislative goals because the agency has the expertise and staffing to fulfill the goals. The agency then creates a detailed plan, sometimes called a regulatory scheme, which fulfills the legislative goals.

When interpreting the law, courts defer to agency expertise.[2] Agency expertise can be found in the rules promulgated by the agency, which often set forth standards or expectations. However, if a conflict arises between an agency regulation or policy decision and the plain language of a statute, the court will ignore the regulation or policy decision in favor of the statute. Statutes have a higher authority, being promulgated by the legislature directly instead of promulgated by an agency at the direction of the legislature.

The Georgia Administrative Procedure Act (A.P.A.) authorizes and sets forth rulemaking and related procedural requirements for most Georgia

---

1. O.C.G.A. §§ 50-13-1 to 50-13-42 (2021).

2. *Albany Surgical, P.C. v. Dep't of Community Health*, 257 Ga. App. 636, 638, 572 S.E.2d 638, 641 (2002).

agencies. The lifecycle of rules in Georgia begins when they are promulgated by agencies. Agencies must provide notice of proposed and final regulations to the Secretary of State.[3] Proposed and final rules are summarized and published in the state *Georgia Government Register*. The *Register* is published by Lexis, fulfilling the Georgia Secretary of State's duty to publish the bulletin.[4] The Office of the Secretary of State is also responsible for updating the *Official Compilation Rules and Regulations of the State of Georgia* to reflect changes to regulations.[5]

However, some agencies are specifically exempted from the Georgia A.P.A.[6] and may have other sources of authority. For example, the Georgia Constitution authorizes the Georgia State Board of Pardons and Paroles. The Georgia State Board of Workers' Compensation was created and authorized to make rules and judgments in a separate part of the state code. When researching an agency's regulations, it is important to remember that the agency may not be subject to the Georgia A.P.A. and publish its own rules and follow its own processes for decision-making. Table 8-1 lists the steps in researching Georgia regulations.

Table 8-1. Steps for Georgia Regulatory Research

1.	Consult the *Official Compilation Rules and Regulations of the State of Georgia* to find the text of the relevant administrative rule(s). If the agency's rules are not included in the *Official Compilation*, consult the agency website for relevant rule(s).
2.	Validate the rules, a two-step process. First, verify that the language of the rule(s) being consulted was the language in effect at the time of the legal issue. Second, verify that the regulation has not been invalidated by later legislation or case law.
3.	If there could be a question about whether the agency acted in the scope of its authority, research case law to determine whether agency acted within scope of the power granted by the legislature. Consult Chapter 7 for information about case law research.
4.	Find agency and judicial decisions applying the rules. Update the cases.
5.	Research other administrative law resources if applicable.

---

3. O.C.G.A. §§ 50-13-4 to 50-13-7 (2021).

4. O.C.G.A. § 50-13-7 (2021).

5. *Id.*

6. O.C.G.A. § 50-13-2(1) (2021).

A. Find and Update the Rules

The first logical step in researching regulations is to identify the relevant rules. After completing the steps to develop a research plan, described in Chapter 2, the researcher is prepared to locate and then update the applicable regulation or regulations.

i. Finding

Locating Georgia agency regulations can be tricky, because not all agencies' regulations are published in the *Official Compilation Rules and Regulations of the State of Georgia,* the official source for regulations issued by agencies and boards in Georgia. The *Official Compilation* is a source for many agency rules, and the agencies not included within the *Official Compilation* generally publish information about their rules and processes on their own websites. This description of finding regulations first focuses on using the *Official Compilation* and then describes using agency websites. If researching in an unfamiliar area of law, however, researchers should consult Georgia-focused secondary source materials.

Historically, the *Official Compilation* was only available in a multi-volume loose-leaf print compilation. It is no longer available for purchase in print, although the University of Georgia Alexander Campbell King Law Library maintains the historical versions in its collection. Instead, there are many ways to access the current rules online. The official version is available through the Secretary of State's website.[7] The rules may also be accessed unofficially through other premium online research tools including Fastcase, Lexis, and Westlaw. Print versions of the prior versions of the *Official Compilation* may be available at Georgia law libraries.

Researchers may locate administrative rules through browsing the *Official Compilation.* When browsing the rules, it is helpful to know that the *Official Compilation* does not follow a strictly alphabetical order. Each agency, or department, is assigned its own number. Once the agency, or department, is identified, researchers can review the table of contents of the *Official Compilation* for the relevant regulations promulgated by an agency.

Another way to search regulations is by keyword. The Help link on the Secretary of State's free public access version of the rules provides guidance

---

7. *Rules and Regulations of the State of Georgia,* https://rules.sos.state.ga.us/gac/ [https://perma.cc/X2A2-ZH24].

about how to construct an effective search.[8] Of course, searching the rules on Fastcase, Lexis, or Westlaw allows researchers to use the natural language or terms and connector search commands from those systems.

As mentioned above, some agencies' regulations are not included in the *Official Compilation*. Unless familiar with whether specific regulations are included in the *Official Compilation*, a best practice is to check the *Official Compilation* first. If not included in the *Official Compilation*, state agency regulations are also not available from premium legal research services.

Another place to find regulations is the agency's own website. Agencies make regulations and other agency materials available on their own sites. This may be true even for agencies with regulations published in the *Official Compilation*. For example, the Georgia State Board of Workers' Compensation provides extensive information on its site, including rules, forms, some decisions, and other helpful information for claimants, employers, and their representatives.[9]

Once the relevant rules are found, updating a regulation is necessary. This assures that the researcher is consulting the regulation that is currently in effect and that the regulation has not been negatively treated by a court. Sometimes a researcher needs to identify a regulation that was in effect at a particular point in time, because the law has since changed.

ii. Updating a Regulation

An initial question when researching is whether the legal issue relates to the law as it existed in a particular point in time, or whether the researcher simply needs to know the state of the law as of today. With that in mind, updating is the process of assuring that the regulation consulted is current as of today. A regulation may be changed, and no longer valid, if a new regulation has amended it, if a statute has reversed it, or if a judicial opinion has invalidated it. For more information about updating to assure a regulation remains valid, consult Chapter 11.

When verifying that a regulation's language is current as of today, the first step is identifying the date which the regulatory language was current through. The Secretary of State's website indicates the regulations are

---

8. *Rules and Regulations of the State of Georgia*, https://rules.sos.state.ga.us/help. aspx [https://perma.cc/UC2V-B7JX].

9. State Board of Workers' Compensation, https://sbwc.georgia.gov/ [https:// perma.cc/ZGK4-MSBV].

"current through Rules and Regulations filed through" and a date. The date listed by the Secretary of State's website is the date after which a researcher needs to look to identify whether the regulation has been amended or eliminated by the agency.

To check whether the regulation has been amended or eliminated since that date, the researcher may consult the *Georgia Government Register*. The *Register* includes proposed and adopted, or final, regulations. Most rules adopted by an agency do not become effective until 20 days after the rule is filed with the Secretary of State.[10] Rules made on an emergency basis are exempt from that waiting period. Filing the regulations with the Secretary of State is a step that occurs prior to publication of the regulation in the *Register*. Because of the potential lag in time between filing of regulations with the Secretary of State and publication of the *Register*, it may also be worthwhile to check the agency website to see if any indication of changes to the regulations is published there as well.

The *Register* is published monthly. It is published in print and available online. The *Register* contents are also available on Fastcase, Lexis, and Westlaw. When using Fastcase, Lexis, or Westlaw, the regulation's "current through" date will likely be earlier than the version on the Secretary of State's website, because the Secretary of State's data is more current. When updating a regulation from a premium research database, it may be less expensive to locate the regulation using the search tools from the premium research database and then update the regulation by navigating to the citation on the Secretary of State's website.

If, when checking the time between the "current through" date and the current date, no changes that have yet not been compiled are identified, then the regulation is current. To find changes not yet compiled, consult the most recent issue of the *Register*. Again, it is worthwhile to check the agency website as well for indication that the regulation had been updated.

Researchers may need to monitor regulations to be aware of changes when they happen. There are a number of tools legal researchers, attorneys, and others use to monitor the Georgia rules for changes. A free way to monitor regulatory changes would be to set up an alert in Google for a specific agency site. An advantage of this approach would be that the search could include the non-agencies that may regulate an area, such as bar admission. A

---

10. O.C.G.A. § 50-13-6 (2021).

disadvantage is that this may produce irrelevant results and take more time to monitor.

Premium services such as Lexis and Westlaw offer the ability to track regulations and see when agencies propose new regulations. Only those agencies which are included in the *Official Compilation* are reflected in the premium tracking services.

The second reason to update a regulation is to verify that the regulation has not been negatively treated by a court. In other words, the researcher should make sure that no court has held the current version of the rule to be unconstitutional, for example. This method of updating is described in detail in Chapter 11.

iii. Identifying Past Regulations

Sometimes a researcher instead needs the prior version of a regulation. When researching the law from a previous time period, researchers need to consult the history of the regulation to identify the date of the required regulation. With that information, researchers may then seek a copy of the regulations as they existed at that time. The Secretary of State's office will provide research assistance on the history of rules according to a published fee schedule.[11] The Georgia Archives is a source of the *Official Compilation* from 1964–2009.[12] The University of Georgia Alexander Campbell King Law Library also has prior versions of the *Official Compilation*, from 1974 through 2013. Prior versions of the *Official Compilation* are available on Lexis from 1991.

Another possible alternate source to locate prior versions of a regulation would be to check the *Georgia Government Register* which contains the synopsis of the final changes made to regulations as required by the Georgia A.P.A.

Figure 8.1 shows the original date of enactment of the regulation, as well as subsequent dates the rule was repealed and a new rule was adopted. To find the regulation as it was in effect in 1992, the version of the regulation to retrieve was adopted February 25, 1986, and effective March 17, 1986. That version of the regulation was in effect from March 17, 1986, through May 31, 2006.

---

11. *Rules and Regulations,* https://sos.ga.gov/index.php/General/rules_and_regulations [https://perma.cc/45ZK-3CAE].

12. *Secretary of State—Administrative Rules and Regulations—Official Compilation Rules & Regulations,* Finding Aids @ Georgia Archives, https://georgiaarchives.as.atlas-sys.com/repositories/2/resources/368 [https://perma.cc/34GD-ZG39].

Figure 8.1. Rule 130-5-.011 Shampoo Equipment[13]

Rules and Regulations of the State of Georgia

Home | Browse | Help | Go to Georgia SOS | Download

Route : GA R&R » Department 130 » Chapter 130-5 » Rule 130-5-.01

Ga. Comp. R. & Regs. r. 130-5-.01 Shampoo Equipment

Georgia Administrative Code
Department 130. RULES OF GEORGIA STATE BOARD OF COSMETOLOGY
Chapter 130-5. SANITATION AND HEALTH

Current through Rules and Regulations filed through February 7, 2022

Rule 130-5-.01. Shampoo Equipment

Shampoo bowls must be thoroughly cleansed and sanitized.

Cite as Ga. Comp. R. & Regs. R. 130-5-.01
Authority: O.C.G.A. Secs. 43-10-2, 43-10-6.
History. Original Rule entitled "Pets" adopted. F. and eff. 6/30/1965.
Repealed: New Rule entitled "Shampoo Equipment" adopted. F. Feb. 25, 1986; eff. 3/17/1986.
Repealed: New Rule of same title adopted. F. May 11, 2006; eff. 5/31/2006.

B. Identifying the Enabling Authority

As discussed, agencies are generally authorized to regulate by the legislature. When researching an area of law governed by regulations, an important question to ask is whether the agency was acting within the scope of its authority in making the regulations. In the rare instance that regulations were authorized by an Executive Order, the question remains whether the agency was acting within the scope of its authority. Some researchers skip this step if it is clear on its face that the agency was acting within its authority in promulgating a regulation and there is no constitutional basis to challenge the regulation.

To determine whether the agency acted within its authority, you must first consult the statutes that have granted the agency authority to act. Each regulation includes a list of the *authority*, or statutes identified by the agency as granting legislative authority for the regulation.

In Figure 8.1, the authority listed for the regulation is O.C.G.A. §§ 43-10-2, 43-10-6. Researchers can consult these statutory sections to confirm whether the agency has authority to promulgate this regulation under those sections. Another source to consider in evaluating whether the agency acted within the scope of its authority are cases interpreting the sources listed as authority. Chapter 11 discusses how to locate cases interpreting a statute.

---

13. Ga. Comp. R. & Regs. r 130-5-.01 (2021), http://rules.sos.state.ga.us/GAC/130-5-.01 [https://perma.cc/Q669-YD9F].

III. Agency Decisions and Executive Actions

In addition to the quasi-legislative action of rule-making, agencies also engage in quasi-judicial action of issuing opinions or judgements. Agencies take quasi-executive action when they make decisions on permit or license applications, for example. The governor also issues executive actions.

A. Researching Agency Judgments or Decisions

Agencies may make judgments or decisions in cases when they apply agency rules or actions and issue opinions. Agencies may have several levels of review in their decision-making. At the first level, the agency may make a determination or decision based on a review of an application or file. Following that determination, there may be a hearing held before an Administrative Law Judge (ALJ). There is no single source that has decisions from all Georgia agencies, though the Georgia A.P.A. requires agencies to make their final orders, decisions, and opinions available to the public for review.[14]

The Office of State Administrative Hearings (OSAH) is an independent office that provides "impartial administration of administrative hearings" consistent with the Georgia A.P.A. requirements. An agency, upon receiving a request from a party for a hearing, refers the case to OSAH. The OSAH ALJ hears the matter and issues an opinion, generally within 30 days.[15] The agency then has 30 days in which to reject or modify the decision, unless the agency extends that period for an additional 30 to 60 days.[16]

The OSAH provides "a sampling of the thousands of OSAH decisions issued each year," on its website, the Administrative Law Report. This site contains selected decisions issued since March 2013.[17] The site also includes select appellate decisions and annual reports. The site may be searched by judge or topic and also includes news about the court.

---

14. O.C.G.A. § 50-13-3(a)(3) (2021).

15. O.C.G.A. § 50-13-41(d) (2021).

16. O.C.G.A. § 50-13-41(d) (2021).

17. *Administrative Law Report: About the ALR*, Georgia Office of State Administrative Hearings, https://administrativelawreport.com/about-the-alr/ [https://perma.cc/U697-QK23].

Premium services such as Lexis and Westlaw offer some opinions or decisions issued by Georgia administrative agencies, including those related to the Judicial Qualifications Commission, Department of Natural Resources, and the Public Service Commission. The services' offerings may not be identical in terms of the types of content and the currency of the content. Researchers will need to review the coverage of each database.

Agencies' may also make their decisions available on their websites. Decisions of some agencies which are available online through agency sites are not also available through the premium databases. These include published decisions of the State Board of Workers' Compensation[18] and the State Board of Education, which decides appeals of decisions issued by local school boards.

B. Researching Attorney General Opinions

A researcher may look for opinions of the Georgia Attorney General for guidance on the application or interpretation of state law as applied by a state agency. Both the official and unofficial versions of the state statutory code include annotations that refer researchers to Attorney General opinions. Not all jurisdictions weigh these opinions heavily, but they are worth considering in Georgia.

The Georgia Attorney General may be described as the attorney for the state, though the Attorney General's duties are broader.[19] The Attorney General is responsible for representing the state in civil and criminal litigation, representing the state in capital felony actions before the Georgia Supreme Court, and providing legal advice to the executive branch.[20] The Governor and the Georgia Attorney General share concurrent authority and "joint responsibility to protect the State's interests in litigation."[21]

The legislature specifically assigned the Attorney General the duty "to give his opinion in writing or otherwise, on any question of law connected with the interest of the state or with the duties of any of the departments."[22] Courts consider opinions of the Attorney General as persuasive authority,[23] which means that courts are not bound to follow the authority. Attorney General

18. State Board of Workers' Compensation, *Published Awards*, https://sbwc.georgia.gov/published-awards [https://perma.cc/EK4V-Q9HC].

19. *Perdue v. Baker*, 227 Ga. 6; 586 S.E.2d 606, 610 (2003).

20. O.C.G.A. § 45-13-3 (2021).

21. *Perdue v. Baker*, 227 Ga. 6; 586 S.E.2d 606, 610 (2003).

22. O.C.G.A. § 45-15-3(1) (2021).

23. *State v. Durr*, 274 Ga. App. 438, 441, 518 S.E.2d 117, 120 (2005).

opinions, like other persuasive authorities, may be used to help a court decide a matter of first impression.

These opinions can be either official or unofficial. The opinions issued specifically at the request of the Governor or the heads of executive departments are official opinions. Unofficial opinions are those issued to other state officers, including legislators, judges, and district attorneys.[24] The Attorney General may also approve or issue other documents, such as interstate compacts or position papers on state law issues.[25]

Researchers can tell the difference between an official and an unofficial Attorney General opinion by the citation. Opinions are numbered by the year and the chronological number of the opinion, separated by a hyphen. Unofficial citations contain the letter "U" in advance of the opinion number. Following is a citation to an official opinion: 2019 Op.Att'y Gen. No. 2019-2, while 2018 Op.Att'y Gen. No. U2018-3 is a citation to an unofficial opinion.

Attorney General opinions may be withdrawn or invalidated by a court opinion or an Act of the General Assembly. Court opinions or legislative action may also modify Attorney General opinions. The Attorney General makes an incomplete list of obsolete or modified opinions available on its website,[26] and notes that "modified opinions should not be disregarded entirely,"[27] but should be read in context. Citators are not available to update attorney general opinions.

Researchers can locate Attorney General opinions using free resources, such as the Office of the Attorney General website, as well as by commercial sources. These sources are listed in Table 8-2. Commercial sources, such as Lexis, Westlaw, and Fastcase, may be available to researchers at libraries or are available through subscriptions. Annotations citing relevant Attorney General opinions are also found in the Official Code of Georgia (O.C.G.A.). Westlaw, an unofficial source of the laws of Georgia, include links to relevant Attorney General opinions as Administrative Decisions & Guidance, when accessed online.

---

24. *Opinions*, Office of the Attorney General, https://law.georgia.gov/opinions [https://perma.cc/Z8NU-SKLQ].

25. *Id.*

26. *Obsolete and Modified Opinions*, Office of the Attorney General, https://law. georgia.gov/obsolete-and-modified-opinions [https://perma.cc/82W7-5U36].

27. *Id.*

Table 8-2. Sources of Attorney General Opinions

Source Name	Web Address	Free or Commercial	Availability
Office of the Attorney General	law.georgia.gov/opinions	Free	1992 to current
Georgia Government Publications	dlg.galileo.usg.edu/ggp/ (search for attorney general opinions and refine by Georgia. Officer of the Attorney General.)	Free	Incomplete collection from 1917 through 2001
Lexis	Lexisnexis.com	Commercial	1839 to current
Westlaw	Westlaw.com	Commercial	1977 to current
Fastcase	Fastcase.com	Commercial	1993 to current
HeinOnline	Heinonline.com	Commercial	1881–current

C. Researching Executive Orders and Proclamations of the Governor

The Governor is the head of the executive branch of government and is empowered to issue executive orders and proclamations. The Governor's proclamations[28] and executive actions, including signed and vetoed legislation and executive orders, are available through the Office of the Governor's website[29] and other sources for the contents of the *Georgia Government Register* listed in Table 8.3.

Unlike proclamations and statements on legislation, executive orders have the force and effect of law. These orders remain in effect until they are rescinded or superseded.[30] Executive orders may have many effects, such as supporting or enforcing existing legislation, or creating commissions. Commissions may make recommendations regarding new laws. Executive orders are published in print in the *Georgia Government Register* and can be found online in the resources in Table 8-3.

---

28. Brian P. Kemp, *Proclamations*, Office of the Governor, https://gov.georgia.gov/contact-us/proclamations [https://perma.cc/5EHA-D7CW].

29. Brian P. Kemp, *Executive Action*, Office of the Governor, https://gov.georgia.gov/executive-action [https://perma.cc/622V-BKT7].

30. *Baxter v. State*, 134 Ga. App. 286, 291–292, 214 S.E.2d 578, 582 (1975).

Using free resources, the easiest way to verify whether an executive order has been superseded is to consult the cumulative index of the *Georgia Government Register*. Citators are not available to update executive orders.

Table 8-3. Sources of *Georgia Government Register*,
Executive Orders, and Proclamations

Source Name	Web Address	Free or Commercial	Notes
Office of the Governor	gov.georgia.gov/ executive-action select Executive Orders; drill down through Governor Nathan Deal's archived site to Governor Sonny Perdue's archived site for orders from 2003 to 2011	Free	2003 to current
Georgia Government Publications	dlg.galileo.usg.edu/ ggp/ search for executive order general opinions and refine by Georgia. Governor and also by Periodicals.	Free	Incomplete collection from 1994 to current
Georgia Government Register	www.plus.lexis.com	Commercial	The issue for a month includes activity from the prior month, ex. December 2020 issue includes orders issued in October and November; 1991 to current

IV. Additional Resources for Researching Georgia Administrative Law

Researchers may choose from a number of sources to research Georgia administrative law questions. One of the most effective starting points is the agency itself. Additionally, Georgia Government Publications is a digital repository for publications of Georgia agencies and the executive branch, as well as Georgia State publications. This section will review each of these sources. Table 8.4 provides information about online sources for state regulations.

Researchers often find agency websites to be highly valuable. In addition to regulations, agency websites may include agency decisions, guidance about agency action, and other resources that may be useful. Agency websites also often contain contact information, meeting schedules, and agendas which are required to be available under Georgia's freedom of information laws.[31] In addition to the decisions and regulations, agency websites often provide interpretive guidance, policies, reports, and other information that researchers may find helpful.

If you are looking to identify Georgia government agencies or other entities, you may do this in several ways. First, you can use a web search engine to identify an agency or entity. You may also consult Georgia.gov, which includes a list of state organizations.[32] The state organizations included on this list are not all technically agencies and thus are not all bound by the Georgia A.P.A. They include significant entities including the Department of Corrections, Employees' Retirement System, and other commissions and councils. The Professional Licensing Boards Division of the Secretary of State's Office assists 42 licensing boards in their work, including hosting websites for the boards and licensing groups.[33] The regulations of these boards are included in the *Official Compilation*. However, not all licensing groups are included. Exceptions include the Office of Bar Admissions, which is an arm of the Supreme Court of Georgia.

The Internet Archive's WayBack Machine is a useful tool for accessing prior versions of agency websites. The Internet Archive includes more than 514

---

31. O.C.G.A. § 50-14-1 (2021).

32. Georgia.gov, *State Organizations*, https://georgia.gov/state-organizations [https://perma.cc/T3RQ-PZTA].

33. Brad Raffensperger, *Licensing*, https://sos.ga.gov/index.php/licensing [https://perma.cc/9N52-SVFX].

billion web pages that have been saved and include, where possible, images, videos, PDF files, and more. When a website is updated, or if its domain name is changed, researchers are still able to glean information from the prior site by consulting the search tool on the WayBack Machine and using the calendar tool to find the date or dates needed. Although not every day for every site is archived, the archive remains helpful and includes almost 25 years of data.

Another good resource for Georgia administrative materials is the Georgia Government Publications database a project of Georgia Library Learning Online (GALILEO). This database provides online access to Georgia agency documents, along with other publications of Georgia including statistical reports and abstracts, budgets, and transcripts of meetings of the Georgia Select Committee on Constitutional Revision. Georgia Government Publications is most effectively searched after reading its Help information, because of the depth of information in the database. Check whether the database allows full text searching. If a database offers full text searching, the search query can be much more detailed than if the database only allows searching of titles, authors, or similar information.

Table 8-4. Sources for Georgia Regulations

Source	Web Address	Free or commercial	Notes
Agency site	Varies	Free	Availability of current and historical regulations varies by agency
Secretary of State	rules.sos.state.ga.us/home.aspx	Free to search	Certified copies and research assistance are available for a fee
Fastcase	Fastcase.com	Free on mobile; commercial on desktop	Included as a benefit of membership to the Georgia Bar
WayBack Machine	archive.org	Free	Use URLs for agency sites to view historical versions.
Bloomberg	Bloomberglaw.com	Commercial	2011 to current
Lexis	Lexisnexis.com	Commercial	2004 to present
Westlaw	Westlaw.com	Commercial	2012 to present

V. Federal Administrative Law

There are many parallels between federal and Georgia administrative law. The federal code and the Georgia code each contain an Administrative Procedure Act (A.P.A.)[34] governing the functioning of agencies and other administrative law issues.

Agencies fulfill their quasi-legislative function in both systems by promulgating regulations, which are then published as proposed regulations and then codified. In both systems regulations should be updated. Also, federal agencies fulfill their quasi-judicial function when they decide cases and issue opinions which are subject to appeal to federal judicial review. Agencies fulfill their quasi-executive function when they enforce regulations and other agency actions. The President, like the Governor, also issues proclamations and executive orders.

A. Federal Administrative Rules

There are two methods of promulgating federal regulations, formal and informal. The formal rulemaking process is similar to a courtroom proceeding, and it is not frequently used. Most federal rules are created by agencies through the informal rulemaking process. This includes three basic steps: (i) notice; (ii) comment period; and (iii) publication.[35] The first step in the process of making federal regulations occurs when new regulations or changes to existing regulations are proposed in the *Federal Register*, which is discussed below.

The next step is the comment period. Typically, regulations need to have at least a 60-day comment period except in cases of emergency. After the comment period, the final regulation is published in the *Federal Register*, taking into consideration public comments provided to the agency.

Proposed regulations, if ultimately finalized in the *Federal Register*, are subsequently codified in the *Code of Federal Regulations*. This section will explain the operation and use of the *Federal Register* and the *Code of Federal Regulations* (C.F.R.).

---

34. *See* Administrative Procedure Act, 5 U.S.C.C § 551 et seq. (2022); Georgia Administrative Procedure Act, § 50-13-1 et seq. (2021).

35. For a more detailed description of the steps of informal rulemaking, see Office of Information and Regulatory Affairs, *FAQs,* https://www.reginfo.gov/public/jsp/Utilities/faq.myjsp [https://perma.cc/L65B-XLFX].

i. Federal Register

The *Federal Register* is published every working day of the federal government and contains more than just administrative rules. It is important in informal rulemaking as the source for rule publication. The informal rulemaking process requires that the public have notice and a meaningful opportunity to be heard regarding proposed regulatory changes.

The *Federal Register* includes proposed rules, final rules, notices from federal agencies and organizations, executive orders and other presidential documents, and finding aids and tools for updating regulations. The *Federal Register* is an official publication of the federal government, published online and in print by the U.S. Government Publishing Office.

The *Federal Register* is published every weekday except federal holidays. Its citation includes both the date of publication and the volume and page number. For example, 85 Fed. Reg. 59,190, September 21, 2020. Because it is paginated consecutively throughout the year, page numbers in the thousands and tens of thousands are common.

The publication of a proposed rule also includes information about the agency, a summary of the proposed rule, helpful supplemental information, and a list of important dates. The deadline for submission of comments, if any, is found in a proposed rule. The publication of the proposed rule and the opportunity for comment upon the rule is the notice and comment process. Most rules go through this informal rulemaking process before they are finalized, the exception generally being those that address exigent, or emergency, circumstances and rules made through formal rulemaking. Formal rulemaking requires hearings and is a less commonly used process of rulemaking.

Final rules are published in the *Federal Register* before they are codified. A final rule includes its effective date as well as a summary of the comments and a description of the agency's consideration of the comments (if there was a notice and comment period). As in Georgia, rules include a list of the statutory or other authority the agency relied upon in promulgating the rules and also include citations to the history of publication for a rule and its amendments, if relevant.

The *Federal Register* may be searched in print, but most people search using an online version. The official version is published by the Government Publishing Office and is available at govinfo.gov. There are other reliable, free versions available on the web, as well as premium access available through legal research vendors. Sources for online access to the *Federal Register* are listed in Table 8-5.

Table 8-5. Sources for the *Federal Register*

Source	Web Address	Description
Govinfo.gov	govinfo.gov	Source of official documents; useful help features
FederalRegister.gov	federalregister.gov	Administered by the National Archives and Records Administration and the GPO, facilitates citizen participation in the regulatory process and decision-making. Contains links to official documents
Regulations.gov	regulations.gov	Online portal for electronic submission of comments on proposed regulations; contains alerting tools
Lexis	Lexisnexis.com	From 1936 to current
Westlaw	Westlaw.com	From 1936 to current
Fastcase	Fastcase.com	Current year
HeinOnline	Heinonline.com	From 1936 to current

ii. The Code of Federal Regulations

Final rules are codified and published in the *Code of Federal Regulations* (C.F.R.). The C.F.R. also includes the authority and history for regulations. The C.F.R.is organized into 50 titles which sometimes, but not always, correspond with the titles in the United States Code. For example, title 26 of the *United States Code* includes the laws related to taxation and title 26 of the C.F.R. includes the regulations issued by the Internal Revenue Service.

When multiple agencies are responsible for administering the law, regulations may be codified in multiple titles. For example, the Wilderness Act is administered by multiple agencies. The regulations authorized under the Act are found in multiple titles of the *C.F.R.*

The C.F.R. is re-published every year, in quarterly installments. This means that the whole set is updated over the course of a year. January 1 is the date the first sixteen titles are revised. Titles 17 through 27 are revised as of April 1. Titles 28 through 41 are revised as of July 1. Finally, the last group of titles, 42 through 50, is revised as of October 1.

Updated titles are not always available on the day they are expected. In print, the updating of a volume is reflected by a change in the color of the cover for the volume. When no change is made to the content of a volume, a new cover is typically stapled to the cover of the old volume. The exception to that practice is title 3, containing presidential documents, which is re-published annually.

Citations for the C.F.R. are formatted as the number of the title, followed by C.F.R., followed by the number of the part, followed by the number of the regulation within the part. For example, 14 C.F.R. 1214.604, enables astronauts to carry personal mementos on space missions. The title is 14, the part is 1214, and the regulation is number 604 within the part.

Researching in the C.F.R. can be done in a variety of ways. The Government Publishing Office (G.P.O.) makes it freely available to search online, as well as available for print research. Table 8-6 contains a list of online sources that can be used to search the C.F.R.

When searching the C.F.R. online, word searching the code database source is one of the most common methods used. Once a relevant regulation is identified, it is particularly important to review the other regulations in the part. They are all part of the same legislative scheme, and they may be helpful to understanding the law relevant to your legal issue.

Whether researchers are using the C.F.R. online or in print they can browse the titles by topic and then review the table of contents to locate relevant regulations. However, researchers need to be familiar with the legal topic in order to use this method because regulations on a legal issue could be found in multiple titles.

Those searching the C.F.R. in print can use an index. The G.P.O. produces an index and other aids that help researchers find regulations based on a statutory authority. *West's Code of Federal Regulations: General Index* is another print index that can help users find regulations related to a legal issue. This is available in Westlaw as well. In addition to the index, another finding aid used to identify additional relevant regulations is the *Parallel Table of Authority and Rules*. The *Parallel Table* is available in print and also online. For information about using it, consult resources listed in Appendix B.

As with other primary sources, when you find a relevant regulation, you will want to verify that the regulation has not been changed. Since the C.F.R. is updated once per year, there is a window of time in which the regulation may be invalidated due to a newly promulgated amendment that has not yet been codified. Also, a court may issue an opinion holding that a regulation lacks proper authority, violates the constitution, or recognizes that a statute contradicts a regulation. These steps are described in Chapter 11, which describes the effective use of citators.

Table 8-6. Sources for the *Code of Federal Regulations* (C.F.R.)

Source	Web Address	Description
Govinfo.gov	govinfo.gov	1996 to present; official source
Fastcase	fastcase.com	2011 to current; unofficial source
HeinOnline	Heinonline.org	1938 to current, unofficial source
Lexis	Lexisnexis.com	1981 to current; unofficial
Westlaw	Westlaw.com	1984 to current; unofficial
eCFR	ecfr.federalregister.gov	Unofficial source for continuously updated version of the C.F.R.; allows for viewing a regulation as it existed at a prior point in time

B. Federal Agencies Make Determinations

In addition to making regulations, an important function of agencies involves *quasi-judicial action*, the determinations that they make. Agencies make decisions or determinations in the context of an application or a conflict with an individual or a corporation. Examples of agency determinations include decisions to issue permits, licenses, or other affirmations of rights such as patents and copyrights or benefits such as Veterans' Benefits or Social Security Benefits. Decisions to levy taxes or to fine behavior by individuals and corporations are also agency determinations.

Agencies begin by taking action in informal proceedings, and these determinations are often made by agency employees after a meeting, application, or similar event. The process of seeking reconsideration of that first informal decision varies from agency to agency. Often, agencies have administrative law judges (ALJs) who may be involved in a hearing and will issue a written opinion. These written opinions are often not aggregated or easily findable, and they have little precedential value. However, they may be useful in advising clients or as persuasive authority. Administrative decisions for select agencies may be available on premium research databases as well as on agency sites.

C. Presidential Actions

The President of the United States issues executive orders and proclamations that have an effect of law. These actions are collected and published in a variety of sources. Executive orders affect the running of the business of government, addressing a variety of topics. Topics addressed in executive orders range from implementing a national HIV/AIDS strategy[36] to amending the rules for civil service employees.[37] Executive orders are numbered in the order that they are issued, and they are published in the *Federal Register* on the day that they are issued. They can be amended by future executive orders.

Another possible type of action is the Presidential Proclamation. Like executive orders, these are numbered in order of issuance and published in the *Federal Register*. Proclamations typically commemorate occasions, such as the death of Representative John Lewis[38] or to promote awareness, such as National Preparedness Month.[39]

In addition to being published in the *Federal Register* and the *Code of Federal Regulations*, these presidential actions are gathered and published in the *Daily Compilation of Presidential Documents*. The compilation also includes signing statements, speeches, nominations to the Senate, press releases, and other materials. All three of these sources are available at govinfo.gov and other premium databases.

---

36. Exec. Order No. 17307, 80 Fed. Reg. 46181 (July 30, 2015).
37. Exec. Order No. 9830, 12 Fed. Reg. 1259 (February 24, 1947).
38. Proclamation 10057, 85 Fed. Reg. 44451 (July 18, 2020).
39. Proclamation 10067, 85 Fed. Reg. 55156 (August 31, 2020).

D. Additional Resources for Researching Federal Administrative Law

As with Georgia, one of the most effective places to consider when researching administrative law issues is the website of the relevant agency. Websites of federal agencies have a wide variety of resources available including agency determinations, interpretations, manuals and related guidance, position statements, news announcements, and forms. These tools can be very valuable to researchers who want to understand or predict agency action for a client. Many agencies' work includes an element of education for the public, which can also provide a researcher with a simple overview of an area of law.

VI. Conclusion

Administrative law research involves the exploration of the work of the executive branch of government, including agencies and the governor or president. Sources of administrative law include regulations, agency determinations, attorney general interpretations, and executive orders. Regulations are the rules which the agency promulgated to govern in the area of law delegated to the agency, while administrative decisions are determinations by the agency in certain circumstances, such as granting or denying a permit, evaluating a claim, or the like.

The workflow for researching Georgia and federal regulations is similar and follows a similar path to other sources. Once the researcher has identified a regulation, the regulation should be evaluated for currentness and validity. If there are questions about agency authority, consult cases interpreting the law. For questions about how the regulation has been implemented, consult administrative decisions and cases. Consult other administrative law resources if applicable.

Chapter 9

Constitutions

After reading this chapter you should be able to:

- Recognize the structure of the Georgia and United States Constitutions; and

- Identify where to access the Georgia and United States Constitutions.

I. Researching Constitutional Law

Researching constitutional law, whether at the state or federal level, can be quite challenging. Although constitutional issues may not arise frequently, researchers must know how to conduct legal research involving constitutional law. Researchers need to rely on secondary sources to understand complex constitutional issues in addition to researching the text and annotations to the Georgia Constitution and the United States Constitution as discussed below.

A. Georgia Constitution

The constitution of the state of Georgia is the highest legal authority for Georgia state law. The Georgia Constitution has gone through ten different revisions. Seven of the revisions were completed through constitution conventions, two were through constitution commissions, and one through the office of legislative counsel of the Georgia General Assembly.[1] The most

---

1. Melvin B. Hill, Jr. & G. LaVerne Williamson Hill, *The Georgia State Constitution* (2d ed., 2018).

recent constitution was ratified during the 1982 election and became effective on July 1, 1983.[2]

The Georgia Constitution consists of a preamble and eleven articles set forth in Table 9-1.

Table 9-1. Articles of the Georgia Constitution

Article	Topic
Article I	Bill of Rights
Article II	Voting and Elections
Article III	Legislative Branch
Article IV	Constitutional Boards and Commissions
Article V	Executive Branch
Article VI	Judicial Branch
Article VII	Taxation and Finance
Article VIII	Education
Article IX	Counties and Municipal Corporations
Article X	Amendments to the Constitution
Article XI	Miscellaneous Provisions

Each of these articles is divided into Sections, Paragraphs, and Subparagraphs. All amendments to the Georgia Constitution must be proposed in the Georgia General Assembly and approved by a two-thirds majority in both the State House and Senate. Amendments must then be passed by a majority of Georgia voters in the next general election. Unlike amendments to the U.S. Constitution, amendments are included/integrated in the appropriate article of the constitution and are not included as separate, numbered amendments.

---

2. *Id.*

1. Georgia Constitution in Print

The Georgia Constitution is located in volume 2 of the Official Code of Georgia Annotated (O.C.G.A.) published by LexisNexis and in volumes 2 and 3 of *West's Code of Georgia Annotated*. As they do for Georgia statutes, editors at LexisNexis and West provide annotations to the paragraphs of the Georgia Constitution. These include case summaries organized by topic and cross-references to applicable primary and secondary sources selected by the editors. The annotations selected by the editors of these publications vary between the O.C.G.A. and *West's Code of Georgia Annotated*.

The most efficient way to research the Georgia Constitution in print is by simply locating the applicable article, section, and paragraph, and then reading the text and annotations. Researchers can locate relevant constitutional provisions by using the statutory indexes located at the end of both the O.C.G.A. and *West's Code of Georgia Annotated* with the terms they developed in their research plan discussed in Chapter 2. Once a relevant paragraph is located, researchers should consult the pocket parts or supplements at the end of the volume(s) to review any new annotations.

Researchers need to use KeyCite in Westlaw and Shepard's in Lexis to ensure the validity of a constitutional provision or identify any pending legislation affecting the provision using the signals set forth in Chapter 11.

2. Georgia Constitution Online

The Georgia Constitution can be found online at the following databases and websites in Table 9-2.

Table 9-2. Georgia Constitution Online

Database or Website	Coverage
Georgia General Assembly (unannotated)	Current
Fastcase (unannotated)	2009, 2013, 2015– Current
Lexis (annotated)	1991–Current
Westlaw (annotated)	2002–Current

The most efficient way to research constitutional provisions is to browse the table of contents in the online database, just as researchers would with a print version of the Constitution. In the online version, researchers may also use keyword or terms and connector searching to locate applicable provisions of the Constitution. Researchers have the option of using an index in Lexis and Westlaw to search for applicable provisions, but other websites and data-bases do not provide an index to their online versions of the Georgia Constitution.

The annotations in Lexis appear at the end of each paragraph contained in the constitution, while annotations appear on the "Notes of Decision" tab in Westlaw. KeyCite and Shepard's permits researchers to review every single case, statute, administrative material, and secondary source included in their respective West and Lexis databases that cite to a paragraph in the Georgia Constitution.

B. United States Constitution

The United States Constitution is the highest legal authority in the United States. The United States Constitution was effective on March 4, 1789, following the ratification of it by a sufficient number of states. The United States Constitution is organized into a preamble, the following seven articles in Table 9-3, a closing endorsement, and the amendments.

Table 9-3. Articles of the United States Constitution

Article	Topic
Article I	Congress
Article II	President
Article III	Judiciary
Article IV	Relations between States
Article V	Amendments
Article VI	Debts Validated, Supreme Law of the Land, Oath of Office
Article VII	Ratification

The United States Constitution is organized by Articles, Sections, and then Clauses. Amendments of the Constitution are arranged separately and currently consist of twenty-seven amendments. The first ten amendments, known as the Bill of Rights, were ratified on December 15, 1791, and added to the Constitution.

1. *United States Constitution in Print*

Table 9-4 shows several sources of the U.S. Constitution in print. The Government Publishing Office also makes the *Constitution of the United States of America: Analysis and Interpretation* available in print and is supplemented annually.

Table 9-4. United States Constitution in Print

Code or Resource	Volume Number(s)
Statutes at Large (unannotated)	1
U.S.C.A. (annotated)	1–31
U.S.C.S. (annotated)	1–14
O.C.G.A. (annotated)	1
West's Code of Georgia Annotated (annotated)	1
Constitution of the United States of America: Analysis and Interpretation (GPO) (annotated)	1

Interestingly, the U.S.C. does not contain the text of the United States Constitution. Researchers seeking the text of constitution within a government publication may consult the *Constitution of the United States of America: Analysis and Interpretation*, made available by the Government Publishing Office (GPO).

The annotated codes in Table 9-4 include case summaries organized by topic and cross-references to applicable primary and secondary sources selected by the editors of the codes. The annotations included in the various annotated codes will vary, and the federal annotated codes will contain more annotations to the United States Constitution than the Georgia codes. Both the U.S.C.A. and the U.S.C.S. have an index to the United States Constitution in the last volume containing the constitution.

Researchers using print versions of the U.S.C.A., U.S.C.S., O.C.G.A. or the *West's Code of Georgia Annotated* will need to review pocket parts and cumulative supplements to ensure that they are not missing any new annotations to the constitutional provisions; Shepard's and KeyCite will contain more up to date annotations for the United States Constitution.

2. *United States Constitution Online*

The United States Constitution can be found online at the following websites and databases in Table 9-5.

Table 9-5. **United States Constitution Online**

Database or Website	Notes
Library of Congress (unannotated)[3]	Statutes at Large Volume 1–18, laws from 1789–1875
govinfo.gov (annotated)[4]	Senate publishes a document entitled Constitution of the United States of America: Analysis and Interpretation
Constitution Annotated	constitution.congress.gov
Fastcase (unannotated)	Within "Constitutions"
Lexis (annotated)	Select "Statutes & Legislation" and then "Constitutions"; not within U.S.C.S. database
Westlaw (annotated)	Within U.S.C.A.

Lexis and Westlaw include annotations, or editorial enhancements, along with the language of the Constitution. Each premium database provider includes summaries of points of law from cases that have interpreted the Constitution, as well as editorial analysis assisting the researcher in finding additional sources. These include selected lists of references as well as exhaustive lists produced using the premium database citators.

C. Conclusion

There are several different ways to access the Georgia and federal constitutions. Researchers should use the annotations and secondary sources to assist them in understanding the constitutional provisions and applying them to their legal issues.

---

3. *Statutes at Large*, Library of Congress, memory.loc.gov/ammem/amlaw/lwsl.html [https://perma.cc/4ELD-B52S].

4. *Constitution of the United States of America: Analysis and Interpretation*, govinfo, govinfo.gov/collection/constitution-annotated [https://perma.cc/WBG5-B5XW].

Chapter 10

Legislative History

After this chapter you should be able to:

- Determine the purpose and weight of legislative history in interpreting statutes;

- Explain the Georgia and federal legislative processes and evaluate the documents produced during legislation; and

- Identify resources for compiled legislative histories and legislative documents.

Legislative history refers to the documents created or considered by the legislature as proposed bills make their way through the legislative process to become laws, if passed. Researchers usually consult legislative history when a statute is not clear on its face and has not been interpreted or analyzed by a court. This chapter provides an overview of the legislative process in the State of Georgia and at the federal level. It then examines the documents produced in during the legislative process and how to use them in order to determine legislators' intent. Finally, this chapter discusses how to track bills of the Georgia General Assembly and of Congress.

I. Weight of Legislative History

Whether interpreting Georgia or federal statutes, it is important to first interpret a statute through its text,[1] cannons of statutory construction,[2] and primary materials[3] that interpret the statute prior to using legislative history

---

1. O.C.G.A. § 1-3-1 (2021); *Williamson v. Lucas*, 171 Ga. App. 695, 697 (1984).

2. *May v. State*, 295 Ga. 388, 391–392 (2014).

3. *Abernathy v. City of Albany*, 269 Ga. 88, 90 (1998); *Schrenko v. DeKalb Cnty. School Dist.*, 276 Ga. 786, 791 (2003).

to interpret a statute.[4] Legislative history materials are not binding on a court; they are persuasive authority. For example, even if a researcher locates a document stating the statute does not apply to "X," a court can ignore this document and apply it to "X" because the document is not mandatory law; it is simply a persuasive argument to the court.

Further, if the research is for a motion before a judge, the researcher should consider how the judge has previously viewed using legislative history in interpreting statutes. Some judges are true textualists and focus on the words of the statute, primary materials, and the cannons of statutory construction rather than try and discern the meaning of a statute from the documents produced during the legislative process. Other judges, such as intentionalists or pragmatists[5] are more likely to consider legislative history in interpreting a statute. Therefore, when trying to assert the legislative body's intent as an interpretation of a statute to a judge, researchers should review previous opinions of the judge to determine the judge's view on using legislative history in a statute's interpretation.[6]

II. Legislative Process in Georgia

Georgia legal researchers benefit from understanding the legislative process in Georgia and knowing the various documents produced during this process. The Georgia General Assembly consists of the Georgia House of Representatives and the Senate. There are 180 members in the Georgia House of Representatives and 56 members in the Georgia Senate. The "General Assembly meet[s] in regular session on the second Monday in January of each year ... and may continue in session for a period of no longer than 40 days in the aggregate each year:"[7] The Georgia legislative process, or the legislative actions from the introduction of proposed legislation to the enactment of a law, is set forth in Table 10-1.

---

4. R. Perry Sentell, Jr., *Georgia Statutory Construction: The Use of Legislative History*, Ga. B.J., Apr. 1996 at 30 (discussing the use of legislative history to interpret statutes in Georgia).

5. Hillel Levin, *Contemporary Meaning and Expectations in Statutory Interpretation*, 2012 Ill. L. Rev. 1103, 1107–14 (2012).

6. For more discussion on this see Valerie C. Brannon, *Cong. Res. Serv., R45153 Statutory Interpretation: Theories, Tools, and Trends*, 37–41 (2018).

7. Ga. Const. art. III, § 4, ¶ I.

Table 10-1. Legislative Process in Georgia[8]

Step	Description
Introduction and First Reading	Legislator files bill with the Clerk of the House or Secretary of the Senate. On legislative day after filing, bill is formally introduced. In chamber, bill's title is read during period of first readings. Immediately after first reading, presiding officer assigns bill to a standing committee.
Second Reading	In the House only, on next legislative day, Clerk reads bill's title (second reading) in chamber, although actual bill is now in committee. In Senate, second reading comes after bill is reported favorably from committee.
Committee Action	Bill considered by committee. Author and other legislators may testify. If controversial, public hearings may be held. Final Committee action reported in a written report. Committee options are:
	Recommend Bill or Resolution Do Pass;
	Recommend Do NOT Pass;
	Recommend Do Pass with changes (amendments or substitutes); or
	Hold Bill.
Third Reading and Passage	Clerk or Secretary prepares a General Calendar of bills favorably reported from committee.
	Legislation which was second read the day before is placed on a calendar in numeric order for floor action prior to the Rules Committee meeting to choose bills for consideration.
	After a certain point, set by rule, the Rules Committee meets and prepares a Rules Calendar for the next day's floor consideration from bills on General Calendar.
	The presiding officer calls up bills from the Rules Calendar for floor action in order as they appear on this calendar.
	Once presiding officer calls bill up from Rules Calendar, Clerk or Secretary reads bill's title (third reading). Bill is now ready for floor debate, amendments, and voting. After debate, main question is called and members vote. If bill is approved by majority of total membership of that house, it is sent to the other house.

---

8. The text of this table is excerpted directly from the General Assembly's website. Georgia Gen. Assembly, *About Legislation*, www.legis.ga.gov/legislation/about [https://perma.cc/K2KR-9GVN].

Transmittal to the Other Chamber	Bill is passed if:
	If the second chamber passes bill, it is returned to chamber where bill was introduced.
	If the first chamber rejects changes and second chamber insists, a conference committee may be appointed. Committee report is accepted by both chambers.
Governor's Signature/Veto	Governor may sign bill or do nothing, and bill becomes law. Governor may veto bill, which requires two-thirds of members of each house to override.
Act	Act and other laws enacted at the session are printed in the *Georgia Laws* series. Also, act is incorporated into the *Official Code of Georgia Annotated*. Laws become effective the following July 1, unless a different effective date is provided in act.

III. Georgia Legislative History Research

Performing legislative history research on Georgia statutes involves looking at the documents and statements produced during the enactment or amendment of a statute to determine the General Assembly's intent behind the statute. Researchers turn to legislative history only when there are questions about the meaning of the statutory language on its face. There are several different resources that researchers can consult to ascertain this intent which are discussed below.

A. Georgia Code

The first place to start in legislative history research is within the Georgia code. The Georgia code contains history information about the statute's enactment and any amendments. This allows researchers to determine when a statute was first enacted and the date of any subsequent amendments. See Figure 10.1. This was discussed in more detail in chapter 4.

Figure 10.1. History Notes in Georgia Statute[9]

History
Ga. L. 1937, p. 746, § 3; Ga. L. 1982, p. 3, § 44; Ga. L. 2016, p. 193, § 7/HB 1004.
OFFICIAL CODE OF GEORGIA ANNOTATED

The researcher can use this information to locate entries in *Georgia Laws*, *Journal of the House of Representatives of the State of Georgia* and the *Journal of the Senate of the State of Georgia* (the *"Journals"*), different versions of the bill, videos of debate on the bill (if any), and secondary sources discussing the enactment or amendment to the statute.

B. Georgia Laws

The text of an act appearing in *Georgia Laws* contains a preamble to the act that discusses the purpose of the statute. This preamble does not appear in codified versions of the act. The provision may be useful to get an overall understanding of the statute's purpose. In the history of the statute depicted above, to view the original enactment of this statute, researchers would need to consult the 1937 volume of *Georgia Laws* on page 746.

The *Georgia Laws* entry includes information on the House or Senate bill number that researchers can then use to find entries in the *Journals*, discussed below. Researchers can find *Georgia Laws* for free in the resources listed in Table 5-1.

C. Journals of the House and Senate

The House and Senate of Georgia produce the *Journal of the House of Representatives of the State of Georgia* and the *Journal of the Senate of the State of Georgia*. These *Journals* are the official compendium of daily records for each chamber. Each *Journal* provides the authors of each measure considered by a chamber, the date of the first and second readings, the name and date of the committee assignment, the committee recommendation, and floor votes. The

9. Source: O.C.G.A. § 44-2-28, www.lexisnexis.com/hottopics/gacode [https://perma.cc/4ZEG-8CZ6].

Journals do not contain the full text of bills or transcripts of floor debates. Unfortunately, most of the information in the *Journals* is not valuable in determining the General Assembly's intent behind a statute.

The most valuable information that the *Journals* provides are the committee and floor amendments and the substitutes to a measure, which can be useful in reviewing amendments to the text, phrases, or provisions in a bill during the legislative process. The *Journals* can be found in print at Georgia law libraries. The print version contains an index where researchers can search by House or Senate bill or by topic. The *Journals* can also be located in Georgia Government Publications[10] in GALILEO, and recent editions of the *Journals* can be found on the Georgia General Assembly website.

D. Versions of Bills

For more recent legislation, researchers can review different versions of a bill to see how it was revised during the legislative process. Researchers can determine if certain words, phrases, or provisions were added or removed from the bill as it moved through the General Assembly. Previous versions of bills going back to 2001-2002 regular session are freely accessible at the Georgia General Assembly website.[11]

E. Video Archives

Even though the General Assembly does not provide transcripts of debates and hearings, for recent legislation, the General Assembly website provides videos of House floor sessions and selected House committee meetings and hearings.[12] Videos for Senate floor sessions and selected Senate committee meetings and hearings are also available on the Senate's Schedule and on the Senate's YouTube channel.[13] Researchers needing access to videos not available online may contact Georgia Archives.

---

10. Digital Library of Georgia, *Georgia Government Publications*, https://dlg.usg.edu/record/dlg_ggpd (select link to view at partner site) [https://perma.cc/8ZA3-K3CU].

11. *Legislation Search*, Georgia General Assembly, www.legis.ga.gov/Legislation/en-US/Search.aspx [https://perma.cc/2R8P-52CN].

12. *House Schedule*, Georgia General Assembly, www.legis.ga.gov/schedule/house [https://perma.cc/2BRB-AGY9]. Videos are also available at the Georgia House of Representatives YouTube channel, www.youtube.com/user/georgiahouseofreps/videos [https://perma.cc/7UX4-C49J].

13. *Senate Schedule*, https://www.legis.ga.gov/schedule/senate [https://perma.cc/K6YL-FLQ8]; *GeorgiaStateSenate*, youtube.com, www.youtube.com/user/Georgia-

F. Secondary Sources

Researchers can consult two secondary sources for Georgia legislative history. The first one is commonly referred to as the "Peach Sheets," published annually in the *Georgia State University Law Review*. The Peach Sheets have been published since 1985 and provide the legislative history of selected acts considered by the Georgia General Assembly. Not every act passed by the General Assembly is included in the Peach Sheets. Peach Sheets are one of the most helpful sources for Georgia legislative history, and judicial opinions cite to the Peach Sheets as an authoritative source.

The Peach Sheets analysis includes previous legislation and other primary law on the legal topic, tracks the bill's progress through the Georgia General Assembly with citations to versions of the bill, citations to the bill in the *Journals*, videos, *Georgia Laws*, and other General Assembly documents. The Peach Sheets also may include various media outlets' references to an act and interviews with legislators. Peach Sheets can be found on the *Georgia State University Law Review* repository.[14]

The other secondary source researchers can consult is the Annual Survey of Law in the *Mercer Law Review*, which has been published since 1950. This survey does not specifically focus on acts passed by the Georgia General Assembly, but it may contain information about certain legislation. The Annual Surveys are available at the *Mercer Law Review*'s website.[15]

G. Online Commercial Databases

Lexis and Westlaw each have databases focusing on Georgia legislative history. However, the coverage of these legislative histories generally begins only after 2003 and may be spotty. Researchers need to review the scope of coverage in these databases when conducting Georgia legislative history research. The Lexis database is called Georgia Legislative Bill History and the West database is called Georgia Legislative History.

StateSenate/featured [https://perma.cc/77DF-VYUB].

14. *Georgia State University Law Review*, Georgia State University College of Law Reading Room, readingroom.law.gsu.edu/gsulr [https://perma.cc/TT6N-R3DG].

15. *Mercer Law Review*, guides.law.mercer.edu/mlr [https://perma.cc/HE5E-4VP8].

IV. Federal Legislative History

Federal legislative history may also be useful in determining the meaning of a federal statutes that is not clear on its face. However, researchers must remember to rely on the text, consult other primary materials, and consider the judge's opinion on using legislative history for statutory interpretation before beginning legislative history research. For researchers, a *compiled legislative history*, one which has been collected and curated by another, is preferable to compiling their own legislative histories.

A. Federal Legislative Process

Just like with Georgia legislative history, it helps to understand the federal legislative process to efficiently conduct legislative history research. There are two legislative bodies in Congress, the House of Representatives, which has 435 members, and the Senate, which has 100 members. The Constitution mandates that Congress meet at least once each year.[16]

A Congress meets for two sessions spanning two years. In January 2021, Congress began the 1st Session of the 117th Congress. The 117th Congress started its 2nd session in January of 2022, and then the 118th Congress starts its 1st Session in January of 2023. Any legislation introduced during a Congress must be passed during that Congress, as any law not passed in a prior Congress must be introduced again to be considered.

The federal legislative process is very similar to the Georgia legislative process. An overview of the legislative process is set forth in Table 10-2.

---

16. U.S. Const. art. 1, § 4.

Table 10-2. Summary of the Federal Legislative Process[17]

Step	Summary	Documents Produced
Introduction	A member of Congress introduces a bill into his or her legislative chamber.	Bills
Referral	The presiding officer of that chamber refers the proposed legislation to one or more committees, depending on its subject.	
Consideration by Committee	Committee members review the bill and decide whether to hold public hearings, to combine it with related draft legislation, the bill to propose amendments, to recommend that the chamber in which it was introduced consider it favorably, or to set it aside for possible later review.	Hearing Transcripts Committee Reports Committee Prints
Floor Scheduling	Majority party leaders generally decide which bills will receive floor consideration.	
Debate and Vote	If the committee, or committees, return the bill to the chamber of the body in which it was introduced, members debate the measure and may consider further amendments. The bill is then voted upon by the entire chamber and transmitted to the other chamber if it passes.	Entries in the *Congressional Record* Amendments to the Bill
Transmittal to the Other Chamber	The bill is then transmitted to the other chamber, where it must go through the same process above.	

---

17. The language of this table is drawn heavily from the following two sources. The United States Capitol Visitor Center provides a simplified statement of how a bill may become a law, while the Congressional Research Service report provides a detailed description of how legislation becomes law. *Cong. Res. Serv. R42843 Introduction to the Legislative Process in the U.S. Congress* (2020); United States Capitol Visitor Center, *Making Laws*, visitthecapitol.gov/about-congress/making-laws [https://perma.cc/7VLE-HH34]. For comprehensive information on the federal legislative process see H.Doc. 110-49 (2007) (How Our Laws Are Made).

Resolving Differences	If a chamber amends the language of the bill, it must go to the other house for concurrence. A conference committee consisting of members of both chambers may be formed to resolve any differences. To move to the next step, both chambers must pass identical versions of the bill.	Conference Reports
President's Signature/ Veto	President has ten days, excluding Sundays, to sign or veto a bill. If the president has not signed the bill after 10 days, it becomes law without his signature. However, if Congress adjourns during the 10-day period, the bill does not become law. If it is vetoed, Congress can only override it by 2/3 majority of each chamber.	Signing State-ments by the President

B. Conducting Federal Legislative History Research

Researchers will find that there are a lot more materials available for federal legislative history research compared to Georgia legislative history research. The federal government publishes the documents listed in Table 10-2. For recent legislation, many are available online.

In most instances Conference and Committee Reports are the most important documents for researchers to consider in their federal legislative history research. These reports likely contain more analysis of a bill than the other documents produced by Congress. However, researchers should also consider other legislative documents if the research project permits because these will provide further context about the legislation.

Reviewing revisions to bills made during the legislative process can assist in determining congressional intent. Normally, during the legislative process particular provisions are eliminated from, or added to a bill, which could signify congressional intent about the legislation in removing or adding that provision. However, researchers should also be aware that the provision could certainly be added or removed for any number of reasons.

Researchers can also review the *Congressional Record* to infer intent. The *Congressional Record* is the official daily record of the debates and proceedings of Congress. This has been published each day that Congress is in session since 1873. The proceedings of Congress were previously recorded in the

Annals of Congress (1789–1824), the *Register of Debates* (1824–1837), and the *Congressional Globe* (1833–1873).

The *Congressional Record* is published in two different formats, the *Congressional Record Daily Edition* and a permanent hardbound edition. The *Congressional Record Daily Edition* consists of four sections listed in Table 10-3. The text of floor debate or speeches appearing in the *Congressional Record* may have been the subject of non-substantive changes prior to publication in both the daily or the permanent publication.

Table 10-3. Sections of the Congressional Record Daily Edition

Section	Description
House Section	Public proceedings and debates of the United States House of Representatives. Each House page will begin with the letter "H" (H2574).
Senate Section	Public proceedings and debates of the United States Senate. Each Senate page will begin with the letter "S" (S2574).
Extensions of Remarks	Supplemental statements made by members of the House and Senate. Each Extension page will begin with the letter "E" (E2574).
Daily Digest (since 1947)	The Daily Digest serves as the table of contents of the Congressional Record even though it is located at the back of each issue. Each Daily Digest page will begin with the letter "D" (D2574).

Once a Congressional session concludes, the Government Publishing Office publishes a permanent hardbound version of the *Congressional Record*. This version consists of one volume for each Congressional session. For example, volume 161 of the *Congressional Record* contains the debates and proceedings of the 1st session of the 114th Congress. The volume contents are organized chronologically. The pagination between the Congressional Record Daily Edition and the permanent edition will vary significantly; HeinOnline's Congressional Record Daily to Bound Locator can be used by researchers to locate a page from the Congressional Record Daily within the bound volume or vice versa. Researchers will know that a citation is to a Daily Digest versus the permanent version by the appearance of "H," "S," "E," or "D" before the page number.

Debates published in the *Congressional Record* may provide some insight, into legislative intent, but the comments from one member of Congress may not reflect accurately the view of the entire House or Senate. Statements by sponsors of the bill or the chair of the committee reviewing the bill during floor debates may be more useful to researchers.

When considering proposed legislation, committees often hold hearings to investigate issues related to the proposed legislation. Transcripts of congressional hearings can be used to show that members of Congress had knowledge about facts or issues involved with the bill. In addition to the transcripts, Congressional hearings may also contain reports, data, investigations, analysis by experts, and other valuable informational resources on the legislation.

Researchers should be wary of relying too heavily on the Extension of Remarks portion of the *Congressional Record* as a reflection of congressional intent. The items included may not actually have been presented as speeches in Congress, but instead have been submitted by request of a Senator or Representative.[18]

Committee Prints are associated materials considered by a committee in conjunction with a bill, including studies, legislative history, and background information. Committee Prints will not be very useful in determining legislative intent, but they are a good source for background information related to the legislation. Finally, Presidential signing statements will not be helpful in determining legislative intent because the president is not a member of Congress.

It can take a lot of work to gather all the documents of a compiled legislative history, especially for bills that are introduced over several sessions of Congress before passing into law. For reasons of efficiency, researchers should look first for a compiled legislative history before creating their own.

C. Compiled Legislative Histories

In some instances, especially for significant acts, like the American with Disabilities Act or the Jumpstart Our Business Startup Act, legislative histories have previously been compiled by researchers. Table 10-4 provides a list of resources that provide compiled legislative histories.

---

18. *Laws and Rules for Publication of the Congressional Record* (Aug. 12, 1986), govinfo.gov/media/RULES.PDF [https://perma.cc/8XM7-GGPN].

Table 10-4. Compiled Legislative Histories

Resource	Description
ProQuest Legislative Insight Part A	A commercial database that covers 18,000 legislative histories of federal laws enacted between 1929–2012 and selected laws enacted prior to 1929.
ProQuest Legislative Insight Part B	Focusing on laws enacted prior to 1929: covers 9,000 legislative histories between 1789–1928 and additional laws from 1929–1965 not included in Legislative Insight Part A
ProQuest Legislative Insight Prospective	New laws from 2013 forward (113th Congress)
HeinOnline — U.S. Federal Legislative History Library	This database in HeinOnline contains sources of previously compiled legislative histories
Ronald E. Wheeler & Jenna E. Fegreus, *Sources of Compiled Legislative Histories: A Bibliography of Government Documents, Periodical Articles, and Books* (2018).	A HeinOnline and print resource of references to compiled legislative histories organized by Congressional session and topic. Scope is from 1st to 114th Congress.
Westlaw — Arnold & Porter Legislative Histories	A Westlaw resource that has selected legislative histories on major acts of Congress.
Westlaw—GAO Federal Legislative Histories	A Westlaw resource for most U.S. public laws enacted between 1921–95 compiled by the Government Accountability Office
Lexis US-CIS-Index (1970–present) and CIS/Historical Index (1789–1984)	Licensed resources that contain legislative histories and an index to congressional publications prepared by the Congressional Information Service.
Legislative Histories of Selected U.S. Laws on the Internet: Free Sources	A free resource provided by the Law Librarians Society of Washington, D.C. that lists free sources of compiled legislative histories
Legislative Histories of U.S. Laws on the Internet: Commercial Sources	A free resource provided by the Law Librarians Society of Washington, D.C. that lists resources to compiled legislative histories in commercial databases.
U.S. Department of Justice (DOJ) Library Staff compilations	Selected legislative histories compiled by the Department of Justice.

Researchers can also review the catalogs of law libraries for resources that compile legislative histories on federal acts.

D. Locating Legislative History Materials Online

If there is not a compiled legislative history available, researchers can use multiple online resources to locate legislative history documents.

One of the best resources available for legislative history research is Congress.gov. Presented by the Library of Congress, the site is a free resource that provides information on legislation going back to 1973. For more recent legislation, Congress.gov links to the hearings, reports, and bills produced as a part of the legislative process. For older legislation, it lists citations to these materials. Researchers can use those citations to obtain the sources elsewhere.

If researchers need to locate legislative history documents, Table 10-5 provides the location of and scope of online sources to the various documents produced during the legislative process.

Table 10-5. Legislative History Documents

Document	Database or website	Coverage
Bills	Congress.gov	Full text of Bills from 1989 to the present; summaries and steps taken in legislative process described from 1799–1873 and 1973 to the present
	Govinfo.gov	From 103rd Congress (1993) to present
	ProQuest Congressional (commercial)	All Congressional bills
Hearings	Congress.gov	Selected hearings from 1995–present
	Govinfo.gov	Selected hearings from 1957–present
	House and Senate Committee websites	Selected hearings
	ProQuest Congressional (commercial)	1824–present
	HeinOnline—U.S Congressional Documents (commercial)	Selected hearings
Committee and Conference Reports	Congress.gov	1995–present
	Govinfo.gov	1995–present
	House and Senate Committee websites	Selected reports
	ProQuest Congressional (commercial)	1824–present
	HeinOnline—U.S Congressional Serial Set (commercial)	1817–present

Congressional Record Daily Edition	Congress.gov	1989–present
	Govinfo.gov	1994–present
	ProQuest Congressional (commercial)	1985–present
	HeinOnline—U.S Congressional Documents (commercial)	1980–present
Congressional Record (permanent)	Congress.gov	1983 to 1994
	Govinfo.gov	1873–to most recent permanent version
	HeinOnline—U.S Congressional Documents (commercial)	1873–to most recent permanent version. Also includes predecessors of the *Congressional Record* (*Annals of Congress, Register of Debates, Congressional Globe*)
Committee Prints	Govinfo.gov	1975–1976, 1989–present
	HeinOnline—U.S Congressional Serial Set (commercial)	1817–present
	ProQuest Congressional (commercial)	1830–present

The resources will also be available in commercial databases such Lexis and Westlaw, but researchers should attempt to use the free resources first. Also, many of these resources may be available in print or microfiche at libraries.

V. Bill Tracking

Instead of looking at the history of a statute, bill tracking involves monitoring the legislation of the current session of a legislative body and tracking the bills as they move through the legislative process. Bill tracking is important to properly advise clients and to keep up to date on the law. Bill tracking for both Georgia and federal legislation can be facilitated through their legislative websites. Premium legal research databases also offer bill tracking features. Lexis and Westlaw offer instructions and support for setting up these features and alerts. It is also possible to set up alerts on some government sites or using search engine features.

A. Georgia General Assembly

The Georgia General Assembly website makes it easy for researchers to track bills in the current session. Researchers can browse and search all bills that have been introduced in the Georgia House or Senate. There also are some specific tools produced by the Georgia General Assembly that can assist researchers in tracking a specific piece of legislation that are described in Table 10-6.

Table 10-6. Georgia Bill Tracking Documents

Document	Summary
Calendars	Both the house and senate issue daily calendars during the legislative session that display current legislation.
Daily Status	This is a daily listing of actions taken on house and senate bills, including first readers, second readers, adopted, favorably reported, and withdrawn.
First Readers	A listing of bills that have had the first reading in the house or senate.
House/Senate Composite Sheets	This is a comprehensive list of the current status of all the bills introduced in the house or senate, from a bill's first reading to the date signed by the governor.
House Daily Reports	A digest of actions taken on bills in the house, including bill summaries, author information, and some committee report information.

Researchers can use the website and these documents to track legislation during any session of the Georgia Assembly. During the Georgia legislative session researchers can also watch *Lawmakers*, which is aired by Georgia Public Broadcasting. This show provides analysis of the legislative session and interviews with members of the Georgia General Assembly.

B. U.S. Congress

Researchers seeking to track federal legislation can use Congress.gov. This website allows researchers to locate legislation by bill number, subject and policy area, status, committee, and other filters. Researchers also have the option to set up alerts for bills introduced on certain topics or changes in status on a certain bill. There are commercial options as well, but researchers may want to try and use Congress.gov to track legislation because it is freely available.

VI. Conclusion

Legislative history is a tool that researchers can use to interpret a statute that is not clear on its face after consulting primary sources such as cases that may have interpreted the statute. However, researchers need to factor in the weight of legislative history in the interpretation of the statute and specifically consider a judge's opinion on using legislative history for statutory interpretation. It is important for researchers to use bill tracking to stay current on the law and to properly advise clients.

Chapter 11

Using Citators

After reading this chapter, you will be able to:

- Define validate;

- Explore how citators appear/function differently on different types of materials;

- Use citators to find more; and

- Describe the role of citators in the research process.

Citators are a valuable tool for legal researchers, providing lists of all the sources that have cited to the law being validated by the citator. The first citators were published in print, but now legal researchers rely on online citators, primarily those of Lexis and Westlaw. When using online citators and related tools, researchers are confirming the validity of the sources they are consulting, identifying whether proposed changes exist for legislative and regulatory sources, and identifying additional sources that are likely relevant and may be of interest. This chapter will address each of those uses for citators and conclude with an exploration of additional tools that researchers may use to evaluate their legal issues. Researchers evaluate the citing references to a case, statute, or a regulation, and consider them independently of the signals offered by online services. Some suggestions for that evaluation are also included.

I. Researchers Validate the Law

Obviously, your argument is strongest when it is based on the current law. To that end, researchers must validate the law before they rely on it. To *validate* a source of law, a researcher checks to see whether another source of law has invalidated, or otherwise modified, the law being relied upon. At the most basic level, this involves verifying whether a case has been reversed or has an appeal pending, which is evaluated by considering the direct history of a case. For statutes or regulations, the basic question is whether the statute or regulation has been amended by a new legislation or rule. Cases, statutes, regulations, and ordinances may be acted upon by other sources of law. The following discussion demonstrates why validation is necessary for each type of law.

A. Cases

The points of law from a case may be invalidated by another court or by a statute. A case can be invalidated by a later ruling from a higher court in the same jurisdiction. That later ruling can hold that the lower court wrongly applied the law, or it can change its interpretation of the law. The later ruling can decline to follow, distinguish, or overrule the lower court's opinion. A later ruling from a different jurisdiction, one in which the original opinion is not controlling, may speak negatively about the original opinion, even though it does not have the authority to change the law as stated in the original case. Citators, which researchers consult to verify the validity of case law, will indicate whether subsequent cases have called into question or invalidated earlier cases.

Note, however, that a holding from a case may also be invalidated by legislative action. In other words, a court may make a statement of law in an opinion and that statement of law may be invalidated by a change of law passed by the legislature. For example, the United States Supreme Court interpreted the Equal Pay Act and Title VII in *Lilly M. Ledbetter v. Goodyear Tire & Rubber Co., Inc.*, 550 U.S. 618 (2007). Congress then passed the Lily Ledbetter Fair Pay Act and invalidated that opinion. The Ledbetter case may be described as "overruled by" or "superseded by" statute.

B. Statutes

Statutes may also be invalidated several ways. A statute may be invalidated by a judicial opinion that holds that the statute violates state or federal constitutional requirements. Because the constitution for a jurisdiction is its highest, most authoritative legal authority, other sources of law may violate constitutional requirements. Courts may decide that statutes violate the constitution.

In addition to checking statutes to see if they are invalid due to a legal decision, it is important to check statutes to see if they have been amended or changed. Typically, researchers seek the current version of a law, although sometimes they seek the law as it existed at a particular time. Those who want the current version of the law must check and make sure that the version being consulted has not been amended or changed since it was published. The citator is a tool that helps with that process. Citators will also indicate whether pending legislation within a jurisdiction may amend the current statute. This will be explained in detail below in section III(B).

C. Regulations

Like statutes, regulations may be invalidated by cases that hold that the regulation is unconstitutional. Additionally, a court may determine that an agency lacked proper authority to promulgate regulations. If a legislature makes a statute that conflicts with a regulation, the regulation is invalidated, or preempted, by the statute. Just as with statutes, researchers typically seek current regulations. An important part of validating a regulation is verifying that the version being consulted has not been amended or changed since it was published.

II. Citators in the Research Process

In addition to consulting citators to assure that the law is "good law," or law which remains valid, researchers often use citators to expand their research and find additional relevant sources. Online citators will only include in their citator reports results that they either publish or license. In other words, if you check the citator on Lexis, its results will not include any sources that are not published or licensed by Lexis. Same thing goes for West-law's citator.

A. Validation in the Research Process

Researchers working online can almost immediately make a preliminary assessment about the validity of a case, statute, or regulation. On the major commercial legal research platforms, statutes, cases, and regulations each include signals indicating at least preliminarily whether the law is valid or if further investigation is needed. For statutes and regulations, researchers can almost immediately determine whether proposed changes are pending as well as whether a court issued an opinion with a negative treatment.

Many researchers rely upon the premium database citator signals early in the research process. They later circle back to evaluate exactly what aspects of a case, for example, are the subject of negative treatment. By making a preliminary review of the source's validity, the researcher is saved from going too far down a path that does not reflect current law. Alternatively, a researcher may review citator signals and choose early in the process to more deeply investigate only those sources signaled as needing greater analysis. The process of thoroughly validating specific source types, as one would need to do when reviewing a citator analysis, is described in Part III of this chapter.

B. Expanding Your Research

In addition to validation, citators play a huge role in helping researchers identify more—more of all types of information! Citators on Lexis and Westlaw include references to the cited, or underlying, source that may be found in court filings, cases, statutes, regulations, treatises, encyclopedias, journals and law review articles, and other sources. From one statute, case, or regulation, it is possible to find many more sources that have cited to the one statute, case, or regulation. Presumably those citing sources would have some relevance to the legal issues of interest.

Researchers may find citators especially helpful for expanding their research when they are starting with a known citation to a primary source. Citator results may include a secondary source or will otherwise recommend secondary sources. Those sources often provide an overview of an area of law, giving researchers more context in which to understand the sources identified in the research process.

When expanding research, it is helpful to consult all the citators you have access to. Lexis and Westlaw will provide similar results, where they have content in common in their databases. However, because the companies' editors are following different guidelines and their services offer some differing secondary sources, there are often differences in the contents of their citator. For this reason, it is beneficial to check citators on both Lexis and Westlaw if available.

BCite, Bloomberg Law's citator for cases, permits researchers to expand their research by identifying other cases that have cited to a case. BCite also provides citations to all primary and secondary materials in Bloomberg Law that cite to a case. Bloomberg's Smart Code allows researchers to locate court decisions that cite to a statute or regulation, but it does not include references to other primary or secondary materials.

When researchers evaluate a case using Fastcase's Authority Check, the results include a list of citing cases. The results also include a timeline with circles indicating the levels of court and frequency of citations from each level of court, allowing users to visually identify trends related to the citation of the case being evaluated.

Bloomberg Law, Fastcase, Lexis and Westlaw offer a variety of ways to limit or sort the results in a citator report by particular characteristics, so that the sources identified may be of more assistance to the researcher. These methods are discussed in more detail below, as they are also used in validating a source of law.

III. Validation Using Online Citators

Online citators are available through Bloomberg Law, Fastcase, Lexis and Westlaw. Lexis publishes Shepard's Citations, which was the first significant tool used to update U.S. law. Westlaw developed the KeyCite tool, a competitive product that is exclusively available online. Most recently, Bloomberg Law developed the BCite citator. Attorneys and researchers who use Fastcase see the Authority Check tool, including the Bad Law Bot, and the Interactive Timeline data visualization tool. Shepard's and KeyCite will determine the validity of most types of primary law. Bloomberg's BCite and Fastcase's Authority Check tool in conjunction with its Bad Law Bot will assist researchers in determining the validity of cases. For this discussion, when describing the functionalities of citators that are common across these commercial providers, Lexis, Westlaw, Bloomberg Law, and Fastcase are included as "premium database providers." Individual providers are called out when their services are being uniquely described.

A. Cases

As noted earlier, premium database providers include a signal on the display of a court opinion indicating negative treatment of the case. The signal is a preliminary indicator to the researcher that more attention is needed to evaluate whether the case is still valid law. Shepard's and KeyCite use their editors to assist in determining in whether a case has received negative treatment. BCite and the Bad Law Bot rely on algorithms, or sets of rules, to make these determinations. Thus, because the database providers use their own criteria to make their determinations about whether treatment is negative, as well as the severity of the negative treatment, the publishers may not all offer the same guidance for the same case.[1] This is one reason why librarians recommend consulting more than one citator if researchers are able.

i. Treatment by Subsequent Courts

For some cases, premium database providers indicate no negative treatment. If such a case is relevant, researchers treat the case as being valid for purposes of continuing their research and preliminary analysis. The researcher has additional analysis to complete if a preliminary signal provided by the premium database providers is negative.

If there is negative treatment of a case, even by only one premium database provider, a researcher must investigate further. First, the researcher needs to identify what point or points of law from the case the researcher is relying upon for their argument or analysis.

Lexis and Westlaw are especially helpful in this regard, because researchers may consult the headnotes to the case and make note of the headnote number or numbers. If the researcher intends to rely upon the points of law reflected in headnotes 3 and 11 (in either Lexis or Westlaw), it is possible to narrow the results of the citator report on Lexis or Westlaw. The narrowed report would include only cases that have some discussion or treatment referencing those points of law. Remember, that the language and numbering of headnotes is not identical between Lexis and Westlaw, so researchers need to check for relevant headnote numbers in both systems rather than relying on one set of headnote numbers across the two systems.

If a researcher does not have Lexis or Westlaw available, it may still be possible to narrow the citator report in other ways, such as by jurisdiction, type of treatment (negative, positive, or neutral), or by date. By narrowing the report however possible, given the options of the premium database provider being used, it is easier to evaluate the case.

With the narrower report in hand, the researcher may then analyze whether the case remains good law as to the issue of interest to the researcher.

---

1. In a recent study comparing the accuracy of citators offered by premium database providers, Paul Hellyer said, "I found highly inconsistent results and egregious mistakes… The results for all three citators [Shepard's, KeyCite, and BCite] are troubling." Paul Hellyer, *Evaluating Shepard's, KeyCite, and BCite for Case Validation Accuracy*, 110 L. Libr. J. 449, 450 (2018).

If the case appears to be good law at that point, it is reasonable to stop the analysis.

However, sometimes the researcher identifies negative treatment and needs to continue the analysis. When a case being validated has possible negative treatment for a point of law being relied upon, there is still at least one question to consider. Is the source of negative treatment from the same jurisdiction or binding on the case being validated?

Sometimes courts consider persuasive authorities, or cases from other jurisdictions, when assigning a citator treatment to a case. In deciding, the courts may indicate that they "decline to follow" or "distinguish" their case from that persuasive authority. Because the court declined to follow or distinguished the persuasive case, the premium database providers flag the persuasive case as having received negative treatment. However, this negative treatment has no legal significance to the persuasive case. The treatment would be significant if the courts were in the same jurisdiction and the negative treatment came from a higher court.

When a researcher encounters negative treatment from a higher court in the same jurisdiction, it is necessary to consider how to proceed. The stronger the negative treatment, the likelier that the case being analyzed has been invalidated. The resources about persuasive writing, recommended in Appendix B, address the dilemma of how and when to use a case that has received some negative treatment from a binding court.

Authority Check, the tool Fastcase provides to analyze the validity of legal authority works a little differently. Cases which have been identified as having negative treatment include a signal indicating so, prompting researchers to consult the Bad Law Bot. The Bad Law Bot is the algorithm that identifies cases that have negatively treated the case being analyzed. In the results, the Bad Law Bot highlights the negative treatment identified in the citing cases. When using Authority Check, results may be narrowed by jurisdiction and sorted by most recent.

ii. Treatment by Statutes

Statutes do not generally include citations to cases in their text, and as a result they may not appear in a citator report for a case. This is the case even if a statute was passed by a legislature specifically to change the effect of a case, as in the Lily Ledbetter Equal Pay Act example above.

Citators reflect instances when cases have been superseded by statute, because the language of subsequent cases often note that treatment. However, not every case with points of law that are superseded by statute have citator treatment highlighting the change in law. Most often, cases are identified as superseded because a court has cited to an opinion for another reason and indicated in the citation to the opinion "superseded by statute on other grounds." That type of language in an opinion is a tip to the researcher that a part of the opinion has been invalidated and may need further investigation.

iii. *Risk of Negative Treatment*

Lexis and Westlaw recently expanded the signals that they use to warn researchers that cases may not be valid. The signals indicate a risk that a rule of law in an opinion has been overruled or treated negatively, though that specific opinion has not itself been cited and described as overruled by another court. Instead, the specific opinion relies upon an opinion that has been overruled or treated negatively in reaching its conclusion. Based on the stated, or explicit, negative treatment of a case, the Lexis and Westlaw citators identify subsequent cases that relied upon the case that received the explicit negative treatment and mark them with an orange signal indicating that there is a risk that they are overruled. The risk of overruling arises because the subsequent case relied upon a case that has now been invalidated.

Before relying upon a case that has an indicator that it may be at risk of having negative treatment, a researcher needs to explore the reason for the signal warning of the risk. On both Lexis and Westlaw, it is possible to identify the case or cases that form the foundation for the risk and analyze the effects on the case identified as being at risk. This signal is not available in Bloomberg Law or Fastcase.

B. Statutes

When researching statutes, researchers also need to ensure the statute is still good law. Researchers must verify that the statute has not been deemed unconstitutional, void, or invalid by a judicial opinion, or amended by new legislation. Researchers also must check if there is pending legislation that would affect the statute. Lexis and Westlaw's citators extend fully to statutes, providing an assessment regarding pending legislation and validity as well as lists of citing sources. Fastcase includes notes regarding constitutionality following the language of statutes and also annotations of citing cases. Bloomberg Law provides information about cases that have cited and discussed statutory provisions.

Lexis and Westlaw both provide signals that are immediately apparent to researchers viewing their statutes. As with cases, the signals allow the researcher to make preliminary judgments about two aspects of validity: whether a court has invalidated the statute and whether legislation that would amend the statute is proposed or enacted. Lexis and Westlaw both clearly label their signals for each of those aspects. Since Georgia statutes are effective on July 1 unless stated otherwise, there is a window of time between the end of the legislative session and July 1 when a statute may have been amended but not yet reflect that change.

Researchers may rely on a statute that has no negative signals. A negative signal could indicate that legislation has been proposed to amend the statute or that no court has issued an opinion negatively treating the statute. The following discussion describes steps to take if a statute has negative treatment in either aspect of validity.

i. Pending Legislation

If a statute has a signal indicating that proposed legislation is pending, the signal is an indication that the researcher needs to verify that the language of the statute has not been amended. The researcher would want to verify when the proposed amendments were filed and how far the proposed amendment has proceeded in the legislative process. The date of the amendment is important because an amendment may only become law if it is passed in the same Congress in which it was introduced.

A proposed amendment from a prior congressional session that has not been reintroduced in the current session cannot become law. However, once a statute has been flagged for a proposed amendment the flag may remain as a signal to researcher that there has in the past been a legislative interest in changing law.

ii. Validity

If a statute has a signal indicating negative treatment, there are a few steps necessary to validate the statutory language. First, identify the case that is the source of negative treatment and see whether it is from your jurisdiction, and thus controlling. If the case is from another jurisdiction, it is persuasive authority that a court might consider invalidating the statute, but it is not the end of your research analysis.

If the case holding indicates your statute is unconstitutional, for example, and is from your jurisdiction, the next step of your analysis is to check the date of the case and compare that date with the history of the statute. If the statute has not been amended since the case, it is possible that part of the statute (or the rest of the Act it was a part of) may not be enforceable. The researcher may also need to determine, typically by reading the case holding the statute unconstitutional, whether the decision rendered the entire statute unconstitutional, or only certain sections or provisions.

If, however, the statute (or the rest of the Act) was amended after it was found to be unconstitutional, it is possible that the legislature cured the problem with the statute. The researcher's job, then, is to evaluate the opinion holding the statute to be unconstitutional and evaluate whether the amendments adequately addressed the issues of causing the statute to be unconstitutional. A researcher relying upon Fastcase's notes regarding constitutionality will need to follow this same path.

C. Regulations

When researching an area of law, researchers often turn to regulations, and regulations need to be validated in a manner similar to statutes. Regulations are made and updated following a notice and comment process, as described in Chapter 8. Citators from Lexis and Westlaw will signal if a case has invalidated or called into question a regulation or if an amendment has been proposed for a regulation. The next sections will assist researchers in evaluating citator signals regarding proposed amendments to federal regulations and the validity of a regulation. Because not all Georgia rule-making bodies are required to publish their proposed rules in the *Georgia Register*, it is best to check the agency website or consult with the agency directly to confirm that no proposed amendments are pending.

i. Proposed Amendments to Regulations

Lexis and Westlaw citators signal that an agency has proposed an amendment to an existing regulation. Again, this might not present an issue if the researcher is seeking the law at a particular point in time. However, if the researcher is looking for the current law, it is useful to know that the law could be changing in the future. The signal is an indicator of that possibility. The signals of proposed regulatory changes on Lexis and Westlaw are not usually current up to the day the researcher is consulting their databases. There may be a lag of a couple of days.

To address the lag, researchers need to consult the CFR Parts Affected from the *Federal Register*, an updating tool provided by the Government Publishing Office.[2] Georgia does not have a comparable tool. A researcher can search for the title and part of a regulation by date or date range (starting with the date that the regulation is current through on Lexis or Westlaw and ending on the current date) to verify whether any proposed changes have been finalized in the gap of time between the currentness of the regulation as seen on Lexis or Westlaw (or any other source) and the current date.

ii. Validity

Citators for regulations also indicate when cases or statutes have invalidated regulations. For example, cases invalidate or provide negative treatment of regulations when the cases hold that the regulation extends beyond the authority delegated to the agency or violates the constitution. A statute might invalidate a regulation if the two conflict. In a conflict between the language of a statute and of a regulation, the language of the statute would control. The citator will not warn a researcher that a regulation has been invalidated until a source, such as a case, cites the regulation and recognizes that the regulation has been invalidated.

IV. Conclusion

Citators are a critical tool for researchers who need to validate or check to see if another source of law has modified a source of law. Citators do not explain the law, and they are not law themselves. However, researchers find them valuable because they can be used to assure that cases, statutes, and regulations remain valid, or "good law." Researchers, when seeing that a case, statute, or regulation, has a signal indicating negative treatment, need to take appropriate steps to verify that the point or points of law of interest to the researcher remain good law. Citators also help researchers expand the scope of their research by identifying potentially relevant sources which have cited to a law (case, statute, or regulation) known to the researcher.

---

2. The GPO website is: https://www.govinfo.gov/app/cfrparts/month [https://perma.cc/ZGZ2-S99E].

Chapter 12

Legal Ethics

After reading this chapter, you will be able to:

- Explain the role of the State Bar of Georgia in the process of attorney discipline;

- Explain the role of state ethical rules and ABA Model Rules in attorney behavior in Georgia;

- Describe the process of judicial discipline in Georgia; and

- Evaluate the resources and strategies recommended to perform legal ethics research.

Attorneys are expected to follow ethical rules in their professional activities. Similarly, judges are expected to follow ethical rules as well. This chapter describes the ways in which attorneys and judges, as a profession, regulate their professional behavior.

I. Process of Researching Ethics Issues Regarding Attorney or Judicial Ethics

Attorneys began regulating their own professional behavior in the 1800s. Regulation continues today, as does regulation of professional behavior of judges. Researching ethical issues for lawyers and judges involves some of the same steps you are familiar with from general legal research. It can be useful to start in secondary sources to get an explanation of the law generally and to find citations to primary sources. However, when researching professional ethics for judges and attorneys, the sources differ. See Table 12-1 for a list of the steps of legal research for ethics issues.

Table 12-1. Steps of Legal Research for Ethics Issues

1. Identify your issue(s) for investigation.
2. Consult a secondary source such as the *Bloomberg/ABA Lawyer's Manual on Professional Conduct,* if available. If not, skip to the next step.
3. Consult the Georgia Rules for Professional Conduct and identify any relevant rules.
4. Consider consulting the Supreme Court of Georgia opinions regarding disciplinary matters.
5. Consider consulting other jurisdictions or Model rules and interpretations as persuasive authority.

Although the process of ethical research may not differ that much from the process of legal research generally, there are significant differences in the sources. Georgia does not have a state-specific treatise addressing legal ethics. However, there are a variety of secondary sources that are national in scope and would provide help for researchers in this area. A sampling of these resources is included in Table 12-2.

Table 12-2. Select Secondary Sources Useful in Researching Attorney Professional Ethics

Title	Print/ Online	About	Resource Type
ABA/Bloomberg Law Lawyers' Manual on Professional Conduct	Online only	Subscription required, includes explanation and analysis of ethics requirements, full text of ethics opinions and model rules, and recent news highlights.	Treatise, updated regularly
Legal Ethics in a Nutshell	Print/online	Organized by rule, this source provides a plain language overview of the ABA Model Rules and also considers the Restatement of the Law Governing Lawyers, Third.	Introductory guide

Professional Responsibility and Regulation, 2d edition	Print/online	Subscription required for online access. Describes professional responsibilities and ethics requirements, includes information about attorney discipline and a table of cases. Indexed.	Study Guide
Legal Ethics: The Lawyer's Deskbook on Professional Responsibility	Print/online	Subscription required for online access. Describes professional ethics require-ments for attorneys and judges. Includes appendixes with Model Rules and some standards.	Treatise, updated annually[1]

Although tempting to consult resources related to attorney malpractice, that is a different legal topic than legal ethics. In Georgia, malpractice claims against attorneys usually require the claimant to prove the attorney who had been hired failed to exercise ordinary care and by that failure caused an injury.[2] Not all malpractice claims will involve potential ethical breaches by the attorney. As a result, secondary sources about legal malpractice do not address all ethical rules in Georgia. *Georgia Legal Malpractice Law*, for example, may be helpful in explaining conflict of interest considerations, but it does not address all potential attorney or judicial ethics questions.

In this area, evaluating whether a source is mandatory or persuasive is particularly important. Mandatory authority will be any rules of professional responsibility that have been adopted in the jurisdiction. For Georgia, one source of mandatory authority is the Georgia Rules of Professional Conduct (GRPC), discussed more below. Ethics opinions may be mandatory, as discussed below. Finally, orders of the Supreme Court of Georgia are mandatory.

---

1. *ABA/Bloomberg Law Lawyer's Manual on Professional Conduct*, Bloomberg Law, https://pro.bloomberglaw.com/aba-bloomberg-law-manual-professional-con-duct/ [https://perma.cc/RQ88-P4M6].

2. Shari L. Klevens & Alanna G. Claire, *Georgia Legal Malpractice Law* 2022 Edi-tion § 1-1 (2020).

The Supreme Court may order attorney discipline as well as issue Formal Advisory Opinions. Other sources are persuasive.

II. Attorney Regulation

State specific rules for professional conduct are often based on Model Rules produced by the American Bar Association. Rules for conduct are accompanied by interpretive guidance that frequently take the form of example scenarios demonstrating the relevance or applicability of a rule to the scenario. Also, attorneys may consult or consider ethics opinions issued by various authorities in planning or evaluating their conduct. Finally, attorneys may also consult a member of the Office of the General Counsel of the State Bar of Georgia to discuss ethics dilemmas.[3]

A. Georgia and the Model Rules

Georgia, like many other states has adopted its own version of the American Bar Association (ABA) Model Rules of Professional Conduct. The ABA Model Rules reflect the development of ideas about ethical behavior and disciplinary consequences for attorneys over time. The ABA developed Model Rules, and states around the country have adopted the rules in whole or in part, sometimes with variation. The Model Rules do not have any weight as law, but the rules adopted by a jurisdiction are binding. The Georgia rules are called the Georgia Rules of Professional Conduct (GRPC), and they were adopted with minor variations from the ABA Model Rules. The GRPC is a mandatory authority regarding ethical behavior of attorneys in Georgia.

When you consult the GRPC, you will note that individual rules may contain a section called "Comment." That section is interpretive guidance to help you understand the application of the rule to particular situations. The comments are persuasive and not binding authority, even though they are included in the GRPC.

The State Bar of Georgia includes as part of the GRPC advisory opinions (discussed more below in section B), which provide guidance to attorneys about proper professional behavior. Prior to 1986, the State Disciplinary

---

3. *Ethics & Discipline*, State Bar of Georgia, https://www.gabar.org/barrules/ethicsandprofessionalism/ [https://perma.cc/Q3AP-K9CD].

Board issued these opinions. Since then, the Supreme Court of Georgia is authorized and has issued Formal Advisory Opinions that are binding. The prior opinions of the Disciplinary Board that are not obsolete remain persuasive authority.

If the GRPC and advisory opinions do not provide clear guidance, you may consult the ABA Model Rules and ABA ethics opinions. These persuasive authorities are helpful in interpreting the GRPC because the GRPC is based on the ABA Model Rules. If there is no Georgia ethics opinion addressing a question, the ABA ethics opinions may provide persuasive and helpful information.

B. State Bar of Georgia

The State Bar of Georgia is a resource for attorneys and for members of the public. It is a legal entity governed by a Board of Governors. The State Bar fosters duty and service to the public, works to "improve the administration of justice," and "to advance the science of law."[4] To those ends, the State Bar offers programs and publications. The State Bar Client Assistance Program, the State Bar's Fee Arbitration Program, and lawyer assistance programs are all offered by the State Bar. Researchers may find helpful the State Bar's publications including the *State Bar of Georgia Handbook* (Handbook) and the *Georgia Bar Journal*.

The *Georgia Bar Journal*, in addition to publishing articles and practitioner suggestions, includes notices related to the GRPC and advisory opinions. The State Bar of Georgia Formal Advisory Opinion Board drafts Formal Advisory Opinions and seeks comment upon them through publication in the *Georgia Bar Journal*. The Advisory Opinion Board submits Formal Advisory Opinions to the Supreme Court of Georgia, which may issue the opinions, making them binding authority. Opinions that are reviewed and modified by the Supreme Court also are binding. If the Supreme Court of Georgia declines to review a drafted advisory opinion, the opinion is not binding beyond the person who requested the opinion and the State Bar of Georgia. This process is governed by the GRPC.

---

4. Ga. State Bar Rules & Regs., R. 1-103 (2022).

C. Sources for Georgia Rules of Professional Conduct

Researchers have many options for searching the GRPC. Current rules are available at the State Bar of Georgia website, with a simple online search tool available. A handy aspect of this resource is that it also includes access to Advisory Opinions and Formal Advisory Opinions.

The GRPC is also available in print from a variety of sources listed in Table 12-3.

Table 12-3. Sources for Georgia Rules of Professional Conduct

Sources for Georgia Rules of Professional Conduct	Notes
Georgia Bar Journal Directory & Handbook	Consult for historical versions of the GRPC.
Georgia Court Rules and Procedure— State and Federal	Print. Published annually.
West's Code of Georgia Annotated	Includes annotations.
Westlaw	Online. Includes annotations. Historical versions available through 2002.
Lexis	Online. Includes annotations. Historical versions available through 2013.

D. Attorney Discipline

Attorney ethical complaints are investigated and prosecuted by the State Bar of Georgia's Office of the General Counsel. The Rules of Professional Conduct include procedural rules that are followed in disciplinary actions. The Supreme Court of Georgia passes final judgment on contested attorney discipline matters.

The Supreme Court of Georgia is the final arbiter of attorney discipline matters. The Court issues orders including findings of misconduct and related discipline. As a researcher, you may consult the Court's orders to better understand the interpretation and application of the GRPC.

III. Judicial Regulation

Judges in Georgia are also expected to follow professional ethical standards. The Georgia Judicial Qualifications Commission (JQC) is the government entity responsible for the regulation of Georgia judges. A Georgia Constitution amendment created the State of Georgia Judicial Qualifications Commission (JQC) in 1972, and in 2016 the voters amended the Constitution to dissolve the JQC and empowered the General Assembly to create and govern a new JQC. The legislature, in creating the new JQC, passed legislation regarding the power of the JQC, its membership, procedures, and confidentiality.[5] Judges, administrative law judges, those performing judicial functions, and candidates for judicial office are accountable to the JQC for their professional ethical behavior.

A. Georgia Judicial Qualifications Commission

The JQC is empowered to investigate and hold hearings regarding complaints of ethical misconduct by Georgia judges. The JQC makes the Georgia Code of Judicial Conduct (GCJC) and the rules for the JQC available on their website.[6] The GCJC is organized by Canons, or broad statements describing ethical conduct. Each Canon is followed by individual rules, which are specific and related to the Canons. The GCJC also includes commentary for each Canon, as well as Application and Termination sections, and a Preamble and Scope Section. The Canons, Rules, and Terminology and Application sections are binding. Commentary and the Preamble and Scope section are not binding.[7]

The GCJC is also available from premium databases. You may find it helpful to consult the premium databases because they include annotations for the rules, including cases that interpreted the rules and applied them to determine whether judges should be disciplined for their conduct. Although the GCJC was completely revised in 2016, cases decided under prior versions of the GCJC are included in the annotations. Before relying on those cases in

---

5. O.C.G.A. § 15-1-21 (2021).

6. Georgia Judicial Qualifications Commission, *Governing Provisions*, https://gajqc.gov/governing-provisions [https://perma.cc/8XTQ-873F].

7. Ga. Code of Judicial Conduct, *Preamble*, § 3 (2021).

understanding a Canon or Rule, you should verify whether the language of the rule applied in the case has been changed in the current rule.

The JQC provides additional support to Georgia judges regarding professional ethical concerns. They provide a helpline for judges to seek advice, called Director's Opinions, in interpreting the GCJC. A judge cannot rely upon a Director's Opinion to establish a general standard of conduct. However, a judge may argue reliance upon a Director's Opinion as a mitigating factor in a disciplinary proceeding.

The JQC also issues Advisory Opinions about judicial conduct. The Hearing Panel considers Director's Opinions in determining whether it should draft a Formal Advisory Opinion.

As discussed in Chapter 8, agency websites are valuable, and the JQC website is a great example. In addition to providing the Code of Judicial Conduct, the site includes the Rules of the JQC and Formal Advisory Opinions.

B. Judicial Discipline

The JQC receives and investigates complaints about judicial behavior. Investigations of complaints begin with preliminary investigation. A full investigation is not required in all circumstances. Sometimes judges resign during an investigation, for example. The JQC makes available on its website a variety of reports, including, judicial resignations in light of JQC investigation and proposed Formal Advisory Opinions put out for public comment. While ongoing, a full investigation remains confidential.

Following a full investigation, the JQC Director may issue a private admonition or reach a deferred discipline agreement, file formal charges, petition to transfer to incapacity inactive status, refer to another agency, sanction the judge, or resolve the matter by the judge's agreement to resign or retire.[8] If formal charges are filed, they are announced on the JQC website. Formal charges are heard by a hearing panel which makes recommendations to the Georgia Supreme Court.[9]

---

8. Rules of the Jud. Qualifications Comm'n of GA, R. 17(D)(1) (2021) [https://perma.cc/Y43F-ZRTU].

9. Rules of the Jud. Qualifications Comm'n of GA, R. 24(B), (E) (2021) [https://perma.cc/Y43F-ZRTU].

After the Georgia Supreme Court considers cases, it issues written decisions either dismissing them or imposing sanctions. You can find these decisions in the *Georgia Reports*, as well as on the JQC website. Researchers consult these opinions for guidance about judicial professional ethics of judges, including interpretation and application of the GCJC.

Georgia Supreme Court decisions regarding judicial discipline can also be located using the digest tools described in Chapter 7. Commercial databases such as those of Lexis and Westlaw include annotations making it easier for researchers to quickly navigate and understand the decisions.

IV. Conclusion

The State Bar of Georgia regulates attorney behavior, including promulgating rules of professional behavior and disciplining attorneys who violate the Georgia Rules of Professional Conduct (GRPC). Researchers may consult ABA Model Rules on which the GRPC are based to identify additional persuasive resources to aid in rule interpretation. Though the sources may be different than appears to be an extra space between than and when researching other legal issues, researchers benefit from first identifying issues and then consulting secondary sources, as they do in researching other areas of the law.

Chapter 13

Dockets and Analytics

After reading this chapter, researchers will be able to:

- Describe the role of dockets in courts;

- Explain why researchers would find dockets helpful for legal research;

- List sources for docket searching; and

- Explain why attorneys and researchers may seek analytics information about courts.

For every case heard by a court, there is a docket that tells the story of the case. The docket is the chronological listing of all events in a case, including filings and proceedings. Researchers use dockets for a variety of reasons. Sometimes researchers want information about a specific case, while other times the researcher is seeking information from a case that may be useful for another purpose. Researchers may use filings they locate in dockets as templates to use in drafting their own filings or to see other attorney's strategies in similar legal matters. There are a variety of sources for dockets. This chapter considers how dockets are used by attorneys and courts, why researchers may find dockets useful, and describes docket searching.

I. Dockets

When a party files an action with a court, the action is assigned a docket number. The docket is the official record of events in the case. Docket numbers typically include an indication of the year and are sequenced chronologically. Some docket numbers include initials after the numbers as an indication of the referee, magistrate, or judge hearing the case. An example docket number is No. 19-351. That docket number is made of two parts. The first, showing the number 19, reflects the year the case was filed with the court, 2019. The number 351 is the sequence number for the matter filed before the court in the year.

A trial court docket contains a list of the filings in cases, such as complaints, summonses, motions, pleadings, and more. Attorneys may elect, under local rules, to include exhibits with their filings. Exhibits can be almost any sort of document, ranging from a personal diary entry to a collection of scholarly articles written by a witness. Appellate court dockets list filings as well, including briefs, motions, and transcripts from trial proceedings.

Party names, names of attorneys, contact information, dates, and other details may also be gathered from a docket. Many docket systems code entries by the subject matter of the claims, or at least the first claim, in an action. These are often referred to as nature of suit codes. This coding, along with the filings themselves, provide researchers with information about matters. Criminal dockets may include listings of the charges filed against defendants, names of co-defendants and their counsel, information about bail or bond, and relevant dates.

Once a matter is concluded, the docket will indicate its resolution. If a party elects to appeal, the docket will indicate the motion to appeal. The appeal would be assigned a new docket number, as it is filed in a new court.

There are several reasons an attorney would find it useful to consult dockets. Attorneys may consult dockets with a particular client or question in mind. Attorneys consult dockets for general research and for active matters. Attorneys may also consult dockets for reasons related to business development or monitoring information for clients.

A. General Docket Research

Attorneys may consult dockets to do general research, though with a particular client or question in mind. There are several reasons an attorney would find it useful to consult dockets. Dockets are a rich source of *underlying filings*, or documents including pleadings, motions, or briefs, and sometimes transcripts. Thus, attorneys may search and review dockets to identify samples of those documents. Dockets are particularly valuable for researchers working in an area of law where cases frequently settle. Due to the high rate of settlement, there may not be as many published cases interpreting or expanding existing law.

Underlying documents in dockets may also provide an opportunity to evaluate the work of an opposing attorney. Attorneys may also evaluate whether another attorney's filings from a similar type of action would be helpful or beneficial in drafting their own filings.

Dockets, because they are so inclusive, may also be used to identify and evaluate expert witnesses. An expert's scholarship may be attached to a motion to qualify the witness as an expert. It may be possible to evaluate how often an expert has testified, or even to review the transcript of a matter in which the expert has testified in the past.

Attorneys may also search dockets when evaluating potential clients. This evaluation could consider whether there are any potential conflicts based on affiliated parties. Another consideration may be whether the client has been the subject of prior litigation for failure to pay bills.

B. Researching Active Client Matters

Attorneys may consult the dockets for active client matters for a variety of reasons. Docket alerts give attorneys immediate notice when an opposing party has filed a motion in an active matter, maximizing the amount of time available for response. Attorneys may also consult the filings in a matter to verify deadlines and dates, as the document contains orders setting deadlines and dates.

II. Conducting Docket Research

Federal court dockets are easiest to search because they have a more unified system. PACER, Public Access to Court Electronic Records, is the federal government's system for managing cases. State court dockets are available in separate systems, with some states having a single system for all case management and other states having different systems in every county and/or court.

There are so many systems for docket searching that researchers are strongly advised to check multiple docket systems if they want to do a thorough job of researching an issue or question. This is particularly true if searching free online sources for dockets. One free source may not have the same underlying filings as another source. It is also possible that one source may include a complete docket sheet with no links to underlying filings, but another source may provide access to underlying filings as well.

One tip researchers should keep in mind is that dockets, like cases, can be current or out of date. In other words, researchers need to evaluate dockets as to whether the docket information is current. Some dockets are retrieved initially by database providers when actions are filed and may not reflect any subsequent filings or court actions. Dockets provided directly from court websites are generally current, but docket information gathered from private docket services may not be current and may need to be updated depending on the researcher's purpose in consulting the docket.

When beginning a docket search, the preliminary step is identifying the source to consult. A preliminary question is whether the docket sought is state or federal. The following discussion describes the sources to consult for Georgia and for federal dockets. Note that the availability of historical docket information varies from court to court. Also, some courts archive old dockets, so if a researcher must visit the court in person to see an old docket, it is advised to make arrangements in advance with the court.

A. Georgia Dockets

Georgia has 159 counties, and the counties do not have a unified system for managing court documents. Following are some of the options for docket searching: individual county court dockets, using the PeachCourt docket system, appellate court dockets, and premium legal research databases.

i. Individual County Court Dockets

Clerks of Court maintain the dockets for their courts. Researchers can locate local court dockets on the web by using a search engine and the keywords of the county name and "court docket." Searching local court dockets may be done individually at the court level. Options for search are typically limited in scope, including attorney name, party name, and docket number. Keyword searching and searching the underlying documents in case files is generally not an option when searching individual county court dockets.

The amount of information available through searching varies by county. Some counties, such as Cobb County, provide free online access to underlying filings in actions. Other counties have much more limited information available online and may require researchers to physically visit the courthouse to retrieve copies of underlying filings. Before paying for access to docket filings, it may be worth checking whether the local court docket makes filings available freely.

Docket information may also vary by courts within counties. For example, Fulton County has a Magistrate Court, a State Court, and a Superior Court. Each of those courts has a separate docket system, and each must be checked separately.

ii. PeachCourt

PeachCourt[1] is a resource for searching many Georgia counties at the same time, though few metro-Atlanta counties participate. The docket information available on PeachCourt is based on the information from participating counties. As a result, there may be inconsistencies in search results. For example, a search for open cases may include cases that have not been finally designated as closed in the county of record, even if the case docket indicates a final order was filed and there have been no filings for years.

Anybody can make an account to search PeachCourt. Attorneys use their accounts to efile in participating counties and can pay for extra services, such as docket monitoring to be notified of filings in an action. Searching and viewing dockets is free for anybody with an account, but PeachCourt charges to view underlying filings. Figure 13.1 shows the PeachCourt search page options.

Documents may be retrieved by case number and party name. Search results can be filtered by case number, court, initiation date, and judge's name.

---

1. More information about PeachCourt is available at https://peachcourt.com/ [https://perma.cc/BZ6Q-TZPS].

Figure 13-1. PeachCourt Search Page Options[2]

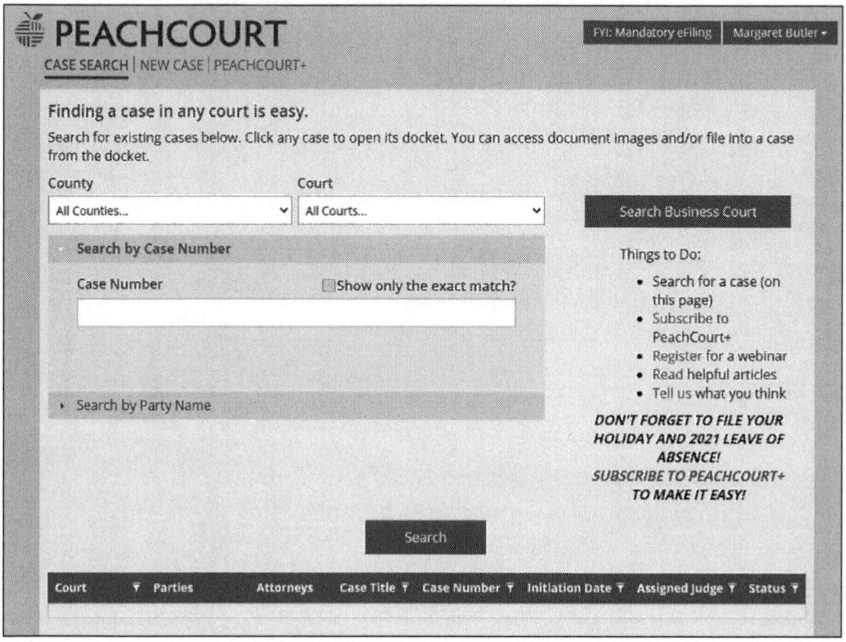

iii. *Appellate Court Dockets*

The Court of Appeals of Georgia docket system contains real time information for court records. Figure 13.2 shows the Court of Appeals Docket Search.
Although the website indicates that information is available only from 2003
on, the system retrieves basic docket information from prior cases.[3] Older
cases do not include working links to access court opinions, however. Available docket information includes the case number, party names (referred to as
the style of the case), attorney names, dates, lower court information, and
information about subsequent history at the Supreme Court, if available.

The options for searching are limited to party names, docket number, and
trial court case number. The Docket/Case Inquiry System also does not

---

2. *Case Search*, PeachCourt, https://peachcourt.com/Search. Used with permission from GreenCourt Legal Technologies.

3. Detailed information about accessing historical court records from 1907–2008
is not available on their website as of this publication. The information remains available through the Internet Archive, https://web.archive.org/web/20210421150217/
https://www.gaappeals.us/locating.php.

display Emergency Motions. To search by date, users need to use a different link on the website. The Court of Appeals of Georgia makes available a glossary of terms that are abbreviated in the docket system.[4]

Figure 13-2. Court of Appeals of Georgia Docket Search[5]

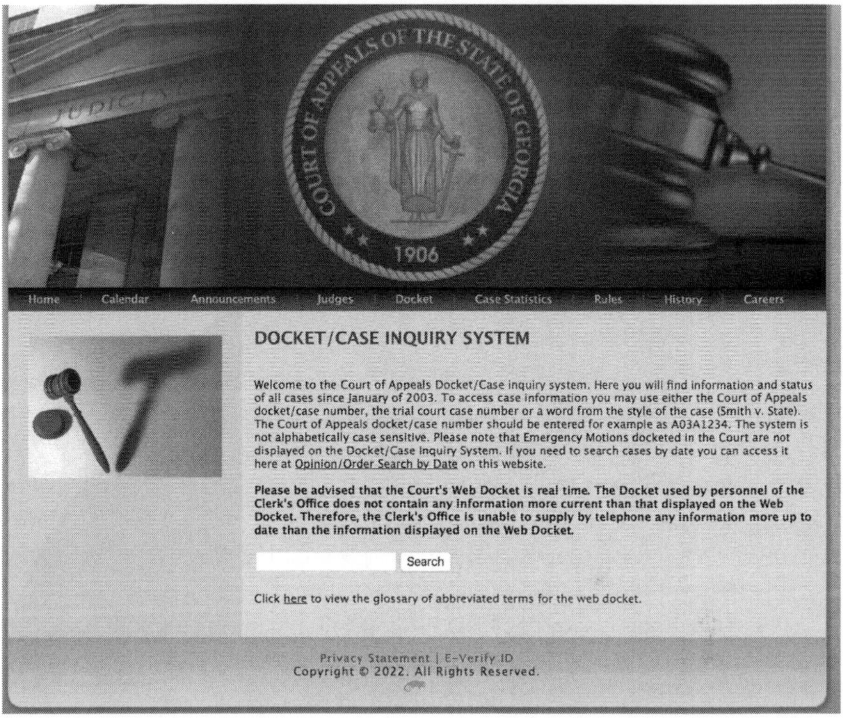

Researchers may search the Supreme Court of Georgia Computerized Docketing System using the Supreme Court case number, an attorney's last name, or the names of parties. The site indicates that the dockets available are from the last three terms of the court.[6] However, a search of the site by party name retrieves five years' worth of filings.

---

4. *Glossary*, Court of Appeals of the State of Georgia, https://www.gaappeals.us/docket/glossary.php [https://perma.cc/FRB4-FZ39]. Used with express permission.

5. *Docket Inquiry System*, Court of Appeals of the State of Georgia, https://www.gaappeals.us/docket/index.php [https://perma.cc/3CCD-RQA9]. Used with express permission.

6. *Computerized Docketing Systems and Case Types*, Supreme Court of Georgia, https://scweb.gasupreme.org:8088/ [https://perma.cc/53VN-HGAH].

The Supreme Court of Georgia docket results do not include links to any of the underlying filings. The dockets contain information about attorneys, descriptions of the matters considered, and notes about the types of proceedings and dispositions. It also fails to provide links within the docket to the opinions issued by the Court. The Supreme Court of Georgia website includes limited access to opinions issued by the court. On Fridays, "Forthcoming Opinions" on the site lists the cases for which opinions will be released the following Monday, if any.[7]

iv. Premium Databases

Premium databases may provide some additional coverage of Georgia trial court dockets. However, that coverage is typically described as "select coverage." Without more details, it is difficult for a researcher to be confident in the scope of the search. Premium databases such as Lexis, Westlaw, and Fastcase often allow more robust searching options than court-run databases, which may be limited to party name or date searching. When searching premium databases, it may be possible to do keyword searching, or to search for statutory provisions. Availability of Georgia appellate court dockets is shown in Table 13-1. Note that Docket Alarm, a Fastcase product, and Bloomberg Law both provide access to search dockets. Docket Alarm does not include dockets at the appellate court level but has significant coverage of trial court dockets.[8] Bloomberg Law provides docket coverage for a variety of Georgia courts, but the extent or scope of coverage varies by court. Scope, or the number of courts included, and extent, or the date range included, of premium database coverage of trial court dockets varies.

---

7. *Forthcoming Opinions*, Supreme Court of Georgia, https://www.gasupreme.us/opinions/forthcoming-opinions/ [https://perma.cc/EG6K-V7G2].

8. *Court Coverage*, Docket Alarm, https://www.docketalarm.com/coverage [https://perma.cc/RH9H-9FEN].

Table 13-1. Georgia Appellate Court Docket Availability

Source	Court	Extent of Coverage
Lexis	Supreme Court of Georgia	Requires CourtLink subscription
	Court of Appeals of Georgia	Requires CourtLink subscription
Westlaw	Supreme Court of Georgia	October 2002 to present
	Court of Appeals of Georgia	October 2002 to present
Supreme Court of Georgia	Supreme Court of Georgia	2003 to present
Court of Appeals of Georgia	Court of Appeals of Georgia	2003 to present (online) 1994–2009 microfilm
Georgia Department of Archives and History	Court of Appeals of Georgia	Pre-1993

B. Federal Dockets

Federal dockets at the trial level are often searched for the variety of underlying filings. Attorneys appreciate the option to consult the work of other attorneys in developing their own arguments and filings. At appellate levels, attorneys often seek information specific to particular judges and their receptivity to arguments as well as arguments that may be used in appellate briefs. This section describes sources useful for docket searching, including PACER, free sites on the web, databases specializing in docket search, and premium legal databases. Docket searching is often done with the goal of reviewing records and briefs related to cases, and sources for those items are also described below.

i. Court Websites

Court websites provide varying access to docket information. Some courts simply link to PACER (see below), while others may provide a list of cases. It is useful to check court websites, if the jurisdiction is known, to confirm a docket number or party name spelling, because those searches are free. Courts may also include access to their opinions.

ii. PACER

The federal government relies on PACER for e-filing, and it is the official system. PACER is always up-to-date and includes the most recent filings in cases. Premium databases that rely on PACER data do not consistently update every case with each new filing. In that respect, PACER has a larger database of underlying filings than premium databases. PACER generally covers from 2001 to present, with earlier case records available from the court directly or through the Federal Records Center of the National Archives. PACER requires an account for searching.

Researchers using PACER are charged fees to search, view results lists, and retrieve underlying filings. Because fees are based on unknown results, the charges associated with PACER may be difficult to predict. However, if a user wants a single filing from a case with a known docket number, it may be that the cost of retrieving the filing will be waived by PACER. Searchers who accrue less than $30 in charges for the previous quarter are not charged.[9]

iii. Free Sites on the Web

Some websites freely available on the web provide docket search databases. CourtListener provides some PACER dockets and documents. CourtListener uses the RECAP Archive in its service. The RECAP Archive is made up of documents that have been downloaded by PACER users who also have an extension on their browser that uploads PACER documents to the RECAP Archive. That means that the RECAP Archive is not as complete as PACER, but its contents are free. Figure 13.3 shows the variety of Search Options in CourtListener, which are more detailed than those available through court websites.

---

9. *PACER Pricing: How Fees Work*, PACER, https://pacer.uscourts.gov/pacer-pricing-how-fees-work [https://perma.cc/29VU-BWRQ].

Figure 13-3. Search Options for CourtListener[10]

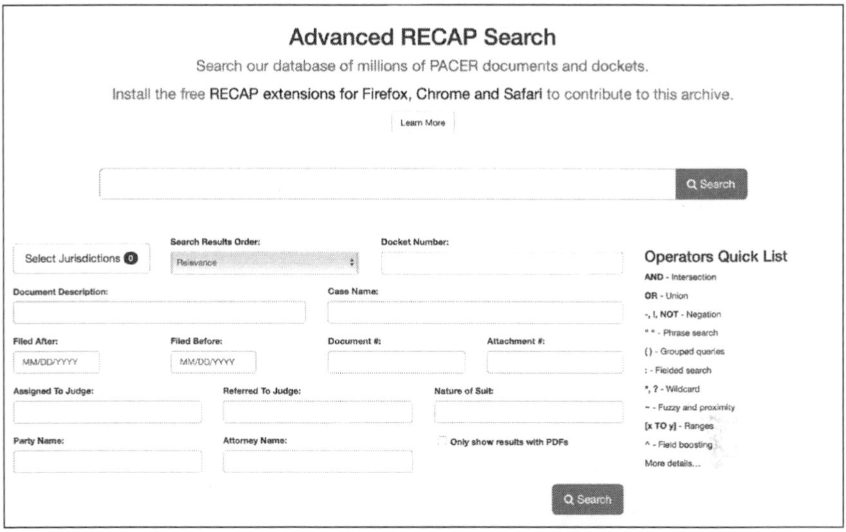

Researchers may also find Justia.com a useful source to search for dockets. Justia provides litigation records from state and federal courts "as a public service."[11] Coverage of federal dockets in Justia is from 2004 to present. Information available through Justia varies from case to case. For some cases, researchers may find only the most preliminary information: case number, file date, court and office, nature of suit, cause of action, and whether a jury has been demanded. For others there may be preliminary information as well as updated dockets and links to documents from the cases. The site includes featured dockets that are newsworthy.

Finally, another useful tool for finding docket or case information is Google. A simple Google search might include party names or a docket number. A more advanced search could include the limitation to search for the file type of PDF. To search by file type, include "filetype:PDF" in the search box. Advocacy organizations and others interested in litigation may post filings or other documents from cases, and they can be found through Google searching.

---

10. *Advanced RECAP Search*, Court Listener, https://www.courtlistener.com/recap/ [https://perma.cc/96HE-6ZHL]. Used with permission.

11. *Dockets and Filings: Why is My Information Online?*, Justia, https://dockets.justia.com/why-is-my-information-online [https://perma.cc/L9TD-4DB3].

iv. Premium Databases Specializing
in Docket Searching

A number of premium databases specialize in docket searching. Premium services include alert tools for monitoring dockets and may also offer users the opportunity to send a runner to a courthouse to get copies of needed court documents. Premium services include CourtLink, a Lexis product, and Docket Alarm, a Fastcase product.

The scope of dockets available through CourtLink varies by court, with more historical docket information available from federal appellate courts than trial courts. Some of the documents that are identified in CourtLink may also be included on Lexis. CourtLink, as a premium docket search product, includes options for users to search by keywords across full text of documents and monitor dockets by setting up alerts. CourtLink includes more than 226 million dockets and documents.

Fastcase offers the product Docket Alarm, which it describes as a "docket research database."[12] Their database is advertised as having more than "400 million briefs, pleadings, motions, and orders."[13] The database has information from federal courts, including specialized courts such as those handling bankruptcy and intellectual property claims. Their search tool allows researchers to search by party names, docket numbers, and legal issues. A variety of filters are also available, including case status, stock symbol, and more.

Docket Alarm includes options for attorneys to set up docket alerts when new filings are made in an open lawsuit. Alerts may also be set up to notify researchers about litigation filed that involves particular parties.

v. Premium Legal Databases

Premium databases such as Lexis, Westlaw, and Bloomberg Law include docket search options that vary significantly by jurisdiction.

Lexis includes docket information for trial courts in Georgia, including some counties that do not participate in PeachCourt. The trial courts

---

12. *Find Briefs, Motions, and Complaints with Docket Alarm*, Fastcase, https://www.fastcase.com/blog/find-briefs-motions-and-complaints-with-docket-alarm/ [https://perma.cc/WGH2-FX8V].

13. *Solo & Small Firm Tools*, Fastcase, https://www.fastcase.com/solo-small-firm/ [https://perma.cc/VA93-GKDR].

available through Lexis are not identified clearly in the information about the databases (separate databases exist for Superior Courts, Magistrate Courts, and State Courts). Also, underlying filings in actions may not be available for researchers through Lexis.

Like Lexis, Westlaw provides some docket search tools for researchers. Westlaw provides dockets information for specified counties, and the availability of historic dockets information varies from county to county.

C. Sources for Records and Briefs

To request discretionary review, the party seeking review files a petition for certiorari. Once certiorari has been granted, parties file briefs with the appellate court. The briefs frame the legal issue and contain a party's argument in support of their position on appeal. Briefs are available as part of the underlying documents in dockets. Briefs may be described as merits briefs or amicus briefs. *Merits briefs* are filed by parties to an appeal and address the merits of the asserted error being reviewed. *Amicus briefs* are also called friend of the court briefs, and they are filed with permission of the court by nonparties seeking to provide the court with additional guidance on the legal issues raised.

Records for cases on appeal are provided to the appellate courts for review. These records, including trial transcripts, exhibit information, and more, may be useful to attorneys or scholars researching or studying cases. Attorneys may find these sources helpful when analyzing claims and planning how to proceed in litigation.

Records and briefs in federal courts, particularly of the United States Supreme Court, are widely available. In addition to accessing information directly from courts, researchers can retrieve records and briefs from particular cases using a variety of sources.

Researchers seeking free information about activities at the United States Supreme Court, including briefs, often start with the court's website. Briefs and other documents are available through case dockets. SCOTUSblog is another source to consult. The SCOTUSblog provides access to briefs from cases starting with October term 2007.

Most premium research databases provide access to merits briefs filed with the United States Supreme Court. These briefs may be found by consulting the case in the database and evaluating the associated filings or by searching each database's collection of U.S. Supreme Court briefs.

III. Legal Analytics

Legal analytics is an area of research in which court and judicial opinion data is analyzed to make predictions related to litigation and planning by lawyers, law firms, and clients. Legal analytics tools use data on judges, courts, attorneys, law firms, expert witnesses, and case types that often has been harvested from dockets. The data used by analytics providers contains information about damages, judges' frequency of granting or denying various types of motions, the time taken to rule on various motions, litigation outcomes (settled, dismissed, verdict, etc.), expert witness challenges, and types of cases. The types of cases information may be derived from nature of suit codes assigned to cases when they are filed.

Analytics may be used to assist researchers on litigation and settlement strategies, advise clients on their legal disputes, select expert witnesses, and choose where to file a lawsuit. Because of its role in decision-making, analytics are sometimes also called "legal intelligence." When relying on analytics to make decisions, researchers and attorneys need to understand whether the data used by the analytics tool is adequate to substantiate the decision. Data may be biased, contain errors due to poor data entry by the source of the underlying data (typically a court docket), and data sets need to be large enough to be valid and reliable.

Premium database providers provide data analytics through their platforms, as do some docket providers. Bloomberg Law provides Litigation Analytics; Lexis provides Context, Litigation Profile Suite, and Lex Machina; and Westlaw provides Litigation Analytics. Data analytics are more robust for federal courts and state appellate courts, but some smaller providers, such as Gavelytics or Trellis are developing analytics products that include data from state trial courts. Fastcase's Docket Alarm includes their Analytics Workbench tool which provides researchers with access to state, federal, and administrative court data.

IV. Conclusion

Dockets contain the record of events and filings in litigation, and researchers and attorneys find them helpful for a variety of reasons. Dockets are maintained by each court in a jurisdiction, and researchers investigating Georgia dockets have a variety of sources to consult in completing their research. Court websites, commercial products such as PeachCourt, and those offered by premium legal research databases including Fastcase, Lexis, and Westlaw, are useful for Georgia dockets information. Federal docket information may be retrieved from premium legal databases as well as PACER, CourtListener, and Justia, as well as from the web.

Legal analytics guide attorneys as they make decisions about litigation and planning based on data from courts. Researchers should understand the data being used to make analytics predictions, so they can assess the validity and reliability of the predictions. Analytics services are available from a variety of providers including premium database providers, Fastcase, and smaller providers as well.

Appendix A

Legal Citation

Legal citation is the process of including references to primary and secondary materials that support your position on a legal issue in both formal and informal legal documents. These legal citations let readers know where the legal materials are located and provide analytical support for your argument(s). There are several different purposes for citation, as listed in Table A.1.

Table A.1. Purposes of Citation[1]

Show the reader where to find the resource
Indicate the weight and persuasiveness of the resource by displaying the jurisdiction, court, date, and/or type of material
Convey the type and degree of support from the resource. Citations may use signals to display whether a resource provides direct support for the proposition, contradicts the proposition, indirectly supports the proposition, or indicate other categories of support
Demonstrate that your legal argument has been well researched
Provide credit to authors who originated the idea you are asserting

There are three different sources for legal citation in the United States that researchers should be familiar with: *The Bluebook*, the *ALWD Guide to Legal Citation*, and jurisdiction specific citation rules and style guides.

---

1. *The Bluebook: A Uniform System of Citation* 1 (Columbia L. Rev. Ass'n et al. eds., 21st ed. 2020); Association of Legal Writing Directors, Carolyn V. Williams, *ALWD Guide to Legal Citation* (7th ed. 2021).

I. *The Bluebook*

The Bluebook is a publication compiled by the editors of the Columbia Law Review, the Harvard Law Review, the University of Pennsylvania Law Review, and The Yale Law Journal.[2] *The Bluebook* provides citation standards for both law review footnotes and for legal memoranda and court documents.

This publication is divided into four parts. The first part is referred to as the "Bluepages" and provides a general overview of citation for different types of materials. The Bluepages' goal is to provide "easy-to-comprehend guidance" for legal professionals and provides citations in the typeface used in legal documents.[3] The second part of *The Bluebook* consists of white pages that provide in-depth rules for legal citation. The examples in this section are printed in typeface conventions used in law journal footnotes. The third part of *The Bluebook* consists of tables to be used in conjunction with *The Bluebook*'s rules. The tables show abbreviations for various words appearing in a citation, which authority to cite, and other information to properly cite resources. The last part is an index that researchers can consult to locate references of how to cite different types of materials.

II. The ALWD Citation Guide

In 2000, the Association of Legal Writing Directors developed the *ALWD Guide to Legal Citation*. The *ALWD Guide to Legal Citation* was created to make it easier to teach and learn *The Bluebook* rules. The *ALWD Guide to Legal Citation* is organized into seven different parts that contain citations for different types of sources, incorporating citations into documents, and appendices with abbreviations and court formats.

III. Local Rules and Style Guides

Researchers also need to be aware of local citation rules and style guides established by courts or states that govern legal citation. These can be found in the Bluepages of *The Bluebook* on BT2.1 (federal courts) & BT2.2 (state courts). The *ALWD Guide to Legal Citation* lists these in Appendix 2.

---

2. For information on the history of *The Bluebook*, see Fred Shapiro & Julie Graves Krishnaswami, *The Secret History of the Bluebook*, 100 Minn. L. Rev. 1563 (2016),

3. *The Bluebook*, *supra* note 1, at 1.

Researchers should consult the most recent version of local rules and style guides to ensure they have not been revised. These local rules and style guides may provide vastly different rules than are set forth in *The Bluebook* and the *ALWD Guide to Legal Citation*.

IV. Georgia Citation Rules

There are three different rules that apply to legal citation in Georgia state courts. The Supreme Court of Georgia requires that "[a]ll citations of authority must be full and complete. Georgia citations must include the volume and page number of the official Georgia reporters. Cases not yet reported shall be cited by the Supreme Court or Court of Appeals case number and date of decision." [4] The rules of the Court of Appeals of Georgia also require citation to the official reporters. [5] Case citations within Georgia courts often provide a parallel citation to the *South Eastern Reporter* so readers can locate the citation within the official Georgia reporter or the *South Eastern Reporter*.

The O.C.G.A. § 1-1-8(e) permits citation to the Official Code of Georgia Annotated as the "O.C.G.A.," while *The Bluebook* and the *ALWD Guide to Legal Citation* abbreviate the Georgia Code as "Ga. Code. Ann." Researchers may see references to the Georgia code in these different formats.

Georgia federal courts also have rules for legal citation. The Eleventh Circuit Court of Appeals requires citation to comply with *The Bluebook* or the *ALWD Guide to Legal Citation* and requires a parallel citation to the regional reporter when a state reporter is cited. [6] The Northern District Court of Georgia addresses citation to federal statutes and regulations but does not discuss citation to cases. [7] The Middle and Southern District Courts of Georgia do not have any specific rules about citation to legal authorities.

Table A.2 shows citation pursuant to local Georgia rules, *The Bluebook*, and *ALWD Guide to Legal Citation* rules.

---

4. Ga. Sup. Ct. R. 22.
5. Ga. Ct. App. R. 24(e).
6. 11th Cir. Ct. App. R. 28-1(k).
7. N.D. Ga. R. 5.1(F).

Table A.2. Example Citations

Georgia Law	Bluebook/ALWD Citation	Georgia Rule
Georgia Constitution	GA. CONST. art. II, § 1, ¶ 2.	No variance
Georgia Statutes (print version published by Lexis)	GA. STAT. ANN. § 7-1-630 (2021).	O.C.G.A. § 7-1-630 (2021).
Georgia Statutes (online)	GA. STAT. ANN. § 7-1-630 (Lexis, through 2021 Regular Session).	O.C.G.A. § 7-1-630 (Lexis, through 2021 Regular Session).
Session Laws	2015 GA. LAWS 758.	No variance
Reported Cases	*Phillips v. Bacon*, 267 S.E.2d 249 (Ga. 1980).	*Phillips v. Bacon*, 245 Ga. 814, 267 S.E.2d 249 (1980).
Unreported Cases	*Wright v. J.H. Harvey Co.*, No. Civ. A. 06V-101, 2006 WL 3193774 (Ga. Super. July 11, 2006).	No variance
Georgia Regulations	GA. COMP. R. & REGS. § 187-3-2.05 (2021).	No variance

This Appendix and the examples shown in Table A.2 are only an introduction to legal citation. Researchers need to be familiar with the rules of citation set forth in *The Bluebook*, the *ALWD Guide to Legal Citation*, as well as local citation rules. Their rules provide the requirements for citation in footnotes and in-text, signals, subsequent history of cases, full and short citations, different types of materials and many others. These will need to be consulted by researchers to ensure they are citing the primary or secondary source properly.

Appendix B

Selected Bibliography

Georgia Research

Leah F. Chanin, *Reference Guide to Georgia Legal History and Legal Research* (Michie Co., 1980).

Leah F. Chanin & Suzanne L. Cassidy, *Guide to Georgia Legal Research and Legal History* (Harrison Co. 1990 & Supp. 1997).

Melvin B. Hill, *The Georgia State Constitution: A Reference Guide* (Greenwood Press 1994).

Nancy P. Johnson, Nancy J. Adams, & Elizabeth G. Adelman, *Researching Georgia* Law (2006 Edition), 22 Ga. St. U. L. Rev. 381 (2005).

Nancy P. Johnson, Nancy J. Adams, & Elizabeth G. Adelman, *Georgia Legal Research* (Carolina Academic Press, 2007).

Nancy P. Johnson, Kreig Kitts & Ronald Wheeler, Georgia Practice Materials: A Selective Annotated Bibliography, in Frank F. Houdek, ed., *State Practice Materials: Annotated Bibliographies* (W.S. Hein, 2006).

Nancy P. Johnson, Ronald Wheeler, *Georgia Practice Materials: An Annotated Bibliography* (American Association of Law Libraries, 2012).

Kristina L. Niedringhaus, Georgia Pre-Statehood Legal Research, in *Prestatehood Legal Materials: A Fifty-State Research Guide, Including New York City and the District of Columbia* (Michael Chiorazzi & Marguerite Most eds., 2005).

Austin Martin Williams, *Researching Georgia Law* (2015 Edition) (31 Ga. St. U. L. Rev. 74 (2015).

General Research (tending to focus on federal material)

J.D.S. Armstrong, Christopher A. Knott, R. Martin Witt, *Where the Law Is: An Introduction to Advanced Legal Research* (5th ed., Thomson/West 2018).

Robert C. Berring & Elizabeth A. Edinger, *Finding the Law* (12th ed., Thomson/West 2005).

Kent C. Olson, *Legal Research in a Nutshell* (13th ed., West Academic Publishing, 2018).

Stephen Elias & Editors of Nolo, *Legal Research: How to Find and Understand the Law* (18th ed., Nolo 2018).

Christina L. Kunz et al., *The Process of Legal Research: Authorities and Options* (8th ed., Aspen Publishers 2012).

Steven M. Barkan, Barbara A. Bintliff, and Mary Whisner, *Fundamentals of Legal Research* (10th ed., Found. Press 2015). Companion volume: *Legal Research Illustrated.*

Kent C. Olson, Aaron S. Kirschenfeld, Ingrid Mattson, *Principles of Legal Research* (West Academic Publishing, 2020).

Amy E. Sloan, *Basic Legal Research: Tools and Strategies* (5th ed., Aspen Publishers 2012).

Specialized Research

Lee F. Peoples, *Legal Ethics: A Research Guide* (2d ed., W.S. Hein 2006).

William A. Raabe, Gerald E. Whittenburg, & Debra L. Sanders, *Federal Tax Research* (7th ed., Thomson/South-Western 2006).

Gail Levin Richmond, Kevin M. Yamamoto, *Federal Tax Research Guide to Materials and Techniques* (11th ed., West Academic, 2021).

Specialized Legal Research (Penny A. Hazelton, ed., Gallagher Law Library, 2014).

Texts on Legal Analysis

Charles R. Calleros, *Legal Method and Writing* (7th ed., Aspen Publishers 2014).

Christine Coughlin, Joan Malmud Rocklin Sandy Patrick, A Lawyer Writes: A Practical Guide to Legal Analysis (3rd ed., Carolina Academic Press 2018).

Linda H. Edwards, *Legal Writing: Process, Analysis, and Organization* (7th ed., Wolters Kluwer 2018).

Linda H. Edwards, *Legal Writing and Analysis* (7th ed., Wolters Kluwer 2018).

Christopher Soper, Christina D. Lockwood, Bradley G. Clary, and Pamela Val Lysaght, *Successful Legal Analysis and Writing: The Fundamentals* (4th ed., West Academic 2017).

Richard K. Neumann, Jr., Ellie Margolis, Kathryn M. Stanchi, *Legal Reasoning and Legal Writing: Structure, Strategy, and Style* (8th ed., Wolters Kluwer 2017).

Laurel Currie Oates & Anne Enquist, Jeremy Francis, *The Legal Writing Handbook: Analysis, Research, and Writing* (7th ed., Wolters Kluwer 2018).

Mary Barnard Ray & Barbara J. Cox, *Beyond the Basics: A Text for Advanced Legal Writing* (3d ed., West Academic 2013).

David S. Romantz & Kathleen Elliott Vinson, *Legal Analysis: The Fundamental Skill* (Carolina Academic Press 1998).

Deborah A. Schmedemann & Christina L. Kunz, *Synthesis: Legal Reading, Reasoning, and Writing* (5th ed., Wolters Kluwer 2017).

Helene S. Shapo, Marilyn R. Walter, & Elizabeth Fajans, *Writing and Analysis in the Law* (7th ed., West Academic 2018).

Timothy P. Terrell, *The Dimensions of Legal Reasoning: Developing Analytical Acuity from Law School to Practice* (Carolina Academic Press 2016).

Appendix C

Georgia Secondary Sources Organized by Legal Topic[1]

Administrative Law

David Shipley, *The Status of Administrative Agencies under the Georgia Constitution*, 40 Ga. L. Rev. 1109 (2006).

Alternative Dispute Resolution

Douglas H. Yarn, *Georgia Alternative Dispute Resolution* (Thomson Reuters 2022). Available on Westlaw.

Banking

Georgia Dept. of Banking and Finance, *Banking-Related Applications Manual* (2021), dbf.georgia.gov/banks-holding-companies/forms-and-applications.

Civil Procedure

Charles R. Adams III & Cynthia Trumboli Adams, *Brown's Georgia Pleading, Practice and Legal Forms Annotated* (Thomson Reuters 2022). Available on Westlaw.

Robert R. Ambler, Jennifer S. Collins, *Georgia Civil Procedure Forms* (LexisNexis 2021). Available on Lexis.

Alston & Bird LLP, *Georgia Appellate Practice Handbook* (Institute of Continuing Legal Education in Georgia 2012).

---

1. Materials are available in print unless otherwise indicated. Online availability through Lexis and Westlaw is noted. These materials were compiled with the assistance of Austin Martin Williams, *Researching Georgia Law*, 31 Ga. St. U. L. Rev. 741 (2015).

Appellate Handbook for Georgia Lawyers (Thomson Reuters 2021–2022).

Michael S. Carlson, Ronald L. Carlson & Julian A. Cook, *Trial Handbook for Georgia Lawyers* (Thomson Reuters 2021–2022). Available on Westlaw.

Lillian N. Caudle & John D. Hadden, *Georgia Magistrate Court Handbook with Forms* (Thomson Reuters 2021). Available on Westlaw.

Charles M. Cork, Christopher J. McFadden, Charles R. Sheppard, Kelly J. Weathers & David A. Webster, McFadden, *Brewer & Sheppard's Georgia Appellate Practice with Forms* (Thomson Reuters 2021). Available on Westlaw.

Jefferson James Davis & Myles E. Eastwood, *Georgia Litigation Forms and Analysis* (Thomson Reuters 2021). Available on Westlaw.

Georgia Procedure (Thomson Reuters 2022). Available on Westlaw.

Hardy Gregory, Jr., *Georgia Civil Practice* (LexisNexis 2021). Available on Lexis.

LexisNexis Practice Guide: Georgia Civil Trial Procedure (LexisNexis 2021). Available on Lexis.

LexisNexis Practice Guide: Georgia Pretrial Civil Procedure (LexisNexis 2021). Available on Lexis.

John B. Manly, Megan U. Manly & Charles R. Sheppard, *Handbook on Georgia Practice with Forms* (Thomson Reuters 2021–2022). Available on Westlaw.

Mary Donne Peters, *The Admissibility of Expert Testimony in Georgia* (Thomson Reuters 2021–2022). Available on Westlaw.

Wayne M. Purdom, *Georgia Civil Discovery with Forms* (Thomson Reuters 2021–2022). Available on Westlaw.

Richard C. Ruskell, *Davis & Shulman's Georgia Practice & Procedure* (Thomson Reuters 2021–2022). Available on Westlaw.

Richard C. Ruskell, *Ruskell's Civil Pleading and Practice Forms for Use with West's Official Code of Georgia Annotated* (Thomson Reuters 2022).

Philip Weltner II, *Georgia Process and Service with Forms* (Thomson Reuters 2021). Available on Westlaw.

Collections

Stuart Finestone, *Georgia Post-Judgment Collection with Forms* (Thomson Reuters 2022). Available on Westlaw.

Daniel F. Hinkel, *Georgia Construction Mechanics' and Materialmen's Liens with Forms* (Thomson Reuters 2021). Available on Westlaw.

Lewis N. Jones & Elizabeth G. Rankin, *Georgia Legal Collections with Forms* (Thomson Reuters 2021). Available on Westlaw.

Commercial Law

James S. Rankin Jr., *Georgia Enforcement of Security Interests in Personal Property with Forms* (Thomson Reuters 2022). Available on Westlaw.

Contracts

John K. Larkins Jr. & John K. Larkins III, *Georgia Contracts: Law and Litigation* (Thomson Reuters 2021). Available on Westlaw.

Construction

T. Bart Gary, *Georgia Construction Law Handbook* (ALM 2021).

Corporations

David Jon Fischer, G. William Speer, Ronald D. Stallings & Walter G. Moeling IV, *Georgia Corporate Forms* (LexisNexis 2021). Available on Lexis.

L. Andrew Immerman & Andrea Lee Lyman, *Georgia Limited Liability Company Forms and Practice Manual* (Data Trace Publishing 2010).

Robert C. Port, *Georgia Business Litigation* (ALM 2022).

James S. Rankin, Jr. & Elizabeth G. Rankin, *Kaplan's Nadler Georgia Corporations, Limited Partnerships, and Limited Liability Companies with Forms* (Thomson Reuters 2021). Available on Westlaw.

Criminal Law and Procedure

Robert E. Cleary, Jr., *Kurtz Criminal Offenses and Defenses in Georgia* (Thomson Reuters 2021). Available on Westlaw.

Robert E. Cleary, Jr., *Molnar's Georgia Criminal Law: Crimes and Punishments* (Thomson Reuters 2021–2022). Available on Westlaw.

Georgia DUI Trial Practice Manual (Thomson Reuters 2021). Available on Westlaw.

Robert Persse, *LexisNexis Practice Guide: Georgia Criminal Law* (LexisNexis 2021) Available on Lexis.

Deborah Mitchell Robinson, *Georgia's Criminal Justice System* (Carolina Academic Press 2020).

Donald f. Samuel, *Georgia Criminal Law Case Finder* (LexisNexis 2021). Available on Lexis.

Donald F. Samuel, & Brian Steel, *LexisNexis Practice Guide: Georgia Criminal Forms* (LexisNexis 2021). Available on Lexis.

George A. Stein, *Georgia DUI Law: A Resource for Lawyers and Judges* (LexisNexis 2021). Available on Lexis.

Ben W. Studdard, *Daniel's Georgia Criminal Trial Practice* (Thomson Reuters 2021–2022). Available on Westlaw.

Ben W. Studdard, *Daniel's Georgia Criminal Trial Practice Forms* (Thomson Reuters 2021–2022). Available on Westlaw.

Damages

Eric James Hertz & Mark D. Link, *Georgia Law of Damages: with Forms* (Thomson Reuters 2021–2022). Available on Westlaw.

Eric James Hertz & Mark G. Bergethon, *Punitive Damages in Georgia* (Thomson Reuters 2021). Available on Westlaw.

Elder Law

Michael S. Reeves & Stephanie F. Brown, *Georgia Elder Care, Long-Term Health Care and Nursing Home Litigation with Forms* (Thomson Reuters 2022). Available on Westlaw.

Employment and Labor

Labor and Employment in Georgia: A Guide to Employment Laws, Regulations, and Practices (LexisNexis 2021). Available on Lexis.

Thomas J. Mew & Brian J. Sutherland, *Georgia Employment Law* (ALM 2020).

James W. Wimberly, *Georgia Employment Law* (Thomson Reuters 2021). Available on Westlaw.

Environmental Law

Georgia Conservation Law Handbook (LexisNexis 2021).

King & Spalding, *LexisNexis Practice Guide: Georgia Environmental Law* (LexisNexis 2020) Available on Lexis.

Ethics/Malpractice

Alanna G. Clair & Shari L. Klevens, *Georgia Legal Malpractice Law* (ALM 2022). Available on Lexis.

Anna C. Clair, J. Randolph Evans & Shari L. Klevins, *The Lawyer's Handbook: Ethics Compliance and Claim Avoidance* (ALM 2013).

Evidence

Ron L. Carlson & Michael Scott Carlson, *Carlson on Evidence Comparing Georgia and Federal Rules* (LexisNexis 2021).

Ron L. Carlson & Michael Scott Carlson, *Carlsons' Guide to Evidence Authentication—Essential Foundations for Georgia Advocates* (LexisNexis 2021).

Neal W. Dickert, *Georgia Handbook on Foundations and Objections* (Thomson Reuters 2022). Available on Westlaw.

John D. Hadden, *Green's Georgia Law of Evidence* (Thomson Reuters 2021–2022). Available on Westlaw.

Michael E. McLaughlin, *Herman and McLaughlin Admissibility of Evidence in Civil Cases: A Manual for Georgia Trial Lawyers* (Thomson Reuters 2022). Available on Westlaw.

Paul S. Milich, *Courtroom Handbook on Georgia Evidence* (Thomson Reuters 2022). Available on Westlaw.

Ana Marcela Rountree, *Agnor's Georgia Evidence* (Thomson Reuters 2021–2022). Available on Westlaw.

Donald F. Samuel, *LexisNexis Practice Guide: Georgia Criminal Evidence* (LexisNexis 2021). Available on Lexis.

Ben W. Studdard, *Daniel's Georgia Handbook on Criminal Evidence* (Thomson Reuters 2021). Available on Westlaw.

Family and Juvenile Law

Edward E. Bates, Jr., *Georgia Domestic Relations Forms* (LexisNexis 2021). Available on Lexis.

Deborah A. Johnson & David A. Webster, *Georgia Divorce, Alimony and Child Custody* (Thomson Reuters 2022). Available on Westlaw.

Randall M. Kessler, *Library of Georgia Family Law Forms* (ALM 2015). Available on Lexis.

Barry B. McGough, *Georgia Divorce* (Thomson Reuters 2021). Available on Westlaw.

Mark H. Murphy, *Georgia Juvenile Practice and Procedure with Forms* (Thomson Reuters 2021). Available on Westlaw.

Boyd Collar Nolen Tuggle & Roddenbery LLC, *LexisNexis Practice Guide: Georgia Family Law* (LexisNexis 2021). Available on Lexis.

Kathy L. Portnoy & Kynna D. Garner, *Georgia Domestic Relations Case Finder* (LexisNexis 2021). Available on Lexis.

Mary F. Radford, *Georgia Guardianship and Conservatorship* (Thomson Reuters 2021–2022). Available on Westlaw.

Forms – General (other forms are within in the legal topics)

Gerald L. Blanchard & Thomson Reuters, *Georgia Forms: Legal and Business* (Thomson Reuters 2021). Available on Westlaw.

General

Georgia Jurisprudence (Thomson Reuters 2021). Available on Westlaw.

Health Law

Georgia Academy of Healthcare Attorneys, *Georgia Hospital Law Manual* (2013).

Insurance Law

J. Stephen Berry, *Georgia Property and Liability Insurance Law* (Thomson Reuters 2021). Available on Westlaw.

John C. Bonnie & Stephen J. Rapp, *LexisNexis Practice Guide: New Appleman Georgia Insurance Litigation* (LexisNexis 2021). Available on Lexis.

Frank E. Jenkins III & Wallace Miller III, *Georgia Automobile Insurance Law Including Tort Law with Forms* (Thomson Reuters 2021–2022). Available on Westlaw.

Jury Instructions

Council of Superior Court Judges, *Suggested Pattern Jury Instructions* (2022). Available on Westlaw and Lexis.

Eleventh Circuit Judicial Council, *Pattern Jury Instructions* (2022), www.ca11.uscourts.gov/pattern-jury-instructions.

Landlord and Tenant

William J. Dawkins, *Georgia Landlord and Tenant: Breach and Remedies, with Forms* (Thomson Reuters 2022). Available on Westlaw.

William J. Dawkins, *Georgia Landlord and Tenant, Lease Forms and Clauses* (Thomson Reuters 2021–2022). Available on Westlaw.

Legislation

Edwin L. Jackson, Mary E. Stakes, & Paul T. Hardy, *Handbook for Georgia Legislators* (Carl Vinson Institute for Government 2020).

R. Perry Sentell, Jr., *Georgia Statutory Construction: The Use of Legislative History*, Ga. St. B.J., Apr. 1996.

Local and State Government

Ted C. Baggett, *Compliance Auditing in Georgia Counties and Municipalities: A Practical Guide to State Laws for Auditors and Local Government Officials* (Carl Vinson Institute for Government 2022).

Handbook for Georgia Mayors and Council Members (Georgia Municipal Association, with Carl Vinson Institute of Government 2012).

Melvin B. Hill & G. LaVerne Williamson Hill, *The Georgia State Constitution* (Oxford 2018).

Real Property

Frank S. Alexander, Sara J. Toering & Sarah Bolling Mancini, *Georgia Real Estate Finance and Foreclosure Law with Forms* (Thomson Reuters 2021–2022). Available on Westlaw.

Kelsey Grodzicki, *LexisNexis Practice Guide: Georgia Real Estate Litigation* (LexisNexis 2021). Available on Lexis.

Russell S. Grove, Jr. & Deborah E. Glass, *Georgia Real Estate Forms* (LexisNexis 2021). Available on Lexis.

Daniel F. Hinkel, *Georgia Eminent Domain* (Thomson Reuters 2021). Available on Westlaw.

Daniel F. Hinkel, *Georgia Construction Mechanics' & Materialmen's Liens with Forms* (Thomson Reuters 2022). Available on Westlaw.

Daniel F. Hinkel, *Georgia Real Estate Sales Contracts* (Thomson Reuters 2021). Available on Westlaw.

Daniel F. Hinkel, *Georgia Real Estate Title Examinations and Closings with Forms* (Thomson Reuters 2021). Available on Westlaw.

Daniel F. Hinkel, *Pindar's Georgia Real Estate Law and Procedure with Forms* (Thomson Reuters 2022). Available on Westlaw.

Mara A. Mooney & Diane M. Hess, *Fundamentals of Georgia Real Estate Law* (Carolina Academic Press 2020).

Seth G. Weissman & Ned Blumenthal, *The Red Book on Real Estate Contracts in Georgia* (Association of Realtors 2021).

Taxes

Georgia Tax Navigator (Bloomberg). Available only on Bloomberg Law.

Georgia State Tax Reporter (CCH).

Georgia State Tax Reporter (Thomson Reuters). Available only on Checkpoint.

Torts and Personal Injury

Robert E. Cleary, Jr., *Eldridge's Georgia Wrongful Death Actions with Forms* (Thomson Reuters 2022). Available on Westlaw.

William V. Custer, IV, *LexisNexis Practice Guide: Georgia Personal Injury* (LexisNexis 2021). Available on Lexis.

David Hricik & Charles R. Adams III, *Georgia Law of Torts* (Thomson Reuters 2021–2022). Available on Westlaw.

Fried Goldberg LLC, *Library of Georgia Personal Injury Forms* (ALM 2020). Available on Lexis.

Michael J. Gorby, *Premises Liability in Georgia with Forms* (Thomson Reuters 2021–2022). Available on Westlaw.

John D. Hadden & Kenneth L. Shigley, *Georgia Law of Torts—Trial Preparation and Practice* (Thomson Reuters 2022). Available on Westlaw.

Frank E. Jenkins III & Wallace Miller III, *Georgia Automobile Insurance Law Including Tort Law with Forms* (Thomson Reuters 2021–2022). Available on Westlaw.

Preyesh K. Maniklal, *Medical Torts in Georgia: A Handbook on State and Federal Law Handbook on Georgia Medical Malpractice Law* (Thomson Reuters 2021–2022). Available on Westlaw.

J. Kennard Neal & Catherine Payne, *Georgia Products Liability Law* (Thomson Reuters 2022). Available on Westlaw.

Houston D. Smith III, *Soft Tissue Injuries in Georgia Including Whiplash, with Forms* (Thomson Reuters 2022). Available on Westlaw.

Wills Trusts, and Estates

Daniel F. Hinkel, *Georgia Probate & Administration with Forms* (Thomson Reuters 2021). Available on Westlaw.

Bentram L. Levy & Benjamin T. White, *Georgia Estate Planning, Will Drafting and Estate Administration Forms* (LexisNexis 2021). Available on Lexis.

Mary F. Radford, *Georgia Trusts and Trustees* (Thomson Reuters 2021–2022). Available on Westlaw.

Mary F. Radford, *Redfearn Wills & Administration in Georgia* (Thomson Reuters 2021–2022). Available on Westlaw.

Workers Compensation

James B Heirs, Robert R. Potter & Todd A. Brooks, *Georgia Workers' Compensation: Law and Practice* (Thomson Reuters 2021–2022). Available on Westlaw.

Jack B. Hood, Benjamin A. Hardy Jr., & Bobby Lee Cook, *Georgia Workers' Compensation Claims with Forms* (Thomson Reuters 2021–2022). Available on Westlaw.

Douglas T. Lay, *Kissiah and Lay's Georgia Workers' Compensation Law* (Lexis-Nexis 2017). Available on Lexis.

About the Authors

Margaret Butler is the Associate Director for Public Services at the Georgia State University Law Library.

Thomas Striepe is the director of the University of Georgia Alexander Campbell King Law Library.

Index